Bearing The Devil's Mark

Matt G. Paradise

A Purging Talon Book

Copyright © 2007 by Matt G. Paradise

Published by Purging Talon
www.purgingtalon.com

ISBN: 978-0-6151-7668-0

All rights reserved. No part of this book may be used or reproduced in any manner whatsoever without written permission from the author, except in the case of brief quotations embodied in critical articles and reviews. For further information, address Purging Talon at info@purgingtalon.com

Cover and Book Design: Matt G. Paradise
Cover Sculpture: "Sigil of Apocalypse" by Diabolus Rex
     www.diabolusrex.com
Front Cover Photo © 2006 Melanie Laetitia Mantis
     www.laetitiasdeath.com
Back Cover Photo: Matt G. Paradise

Printed in the United States of America
First Edition

Acknowledgments

To friends, role models, and worthwhile individuals...

Anton Szandor LaVey, Peter H. Gilmore, Peggy Nadramia, Bryan Moore, Heather Saenz, Nemo, Robert Lang, Diana DeMagis, Colonel Akula, Blanche Barton, Xerxes LaVey, Bill M., Diabolus Rex, Jack Malebranche, James Sass, David Harris, Lady Ygraine, Michael Rose, Chris Xavier, and Kevin Slaughter.

TABLE OF CONTENTS

Preface..i-viii

Further Evidence of the Satanic Age...1
Ego Transference and the Herd...17
Producer or Consumer? Which One Are You?......................................21
Pop Goes The Pretense...25
Absolutes Can Corrupt Absolutely...29
Love Is A Many Conditional Thing..36
Dating Outside Your Race..41
Let's Hear It For Sexual Objectification..46
Absolute Human Companions: A Practical Inquiry.............................49
The Misanthrope's Survival Guide...53
The Internet: Tool of Stratification..60
From Out of the Woodwork..67
Sifting The Ashes of Anton LaVey..71
Rosemary Revisited..74
B-Horror Dates To Dismember..80
The Satanic Side of the Enlightenment..84
Satanism and Racialism..91
If Voting Changed Anything...97
Everybody's Out To Get Me!..99
Bangin' In Littleton..107
Everything I Learned To Hate About People....................................111

The Black Suit In Both Theory and Application............................115
Other People...119
A Night On The Brocken (The Walpurgisnacht Ceremony)............121
Greater Than Sheep Am I, And Smiling..124
To The Devil His Due..128

Appendix...131-176
    I. Essay Source List
    II. Composite Interview
    III. Satanism FAQ
    IV. Suggested Reading
    V. From The Mail Bag
    VI. MGP Media Résumé

"And now I see the face of god, and I raise this god over the earth, this god whom men have sought since men came into being, this god who will grant them joy and peace and pride. This god, this one word: I."

- Ayn Rand

PREFACE

It was a cold December evening in 1983. As a committed bibliophile, I was once again rummaging through the teetering stacks and high, narrow bookcases of Ephraim's used bookstore, a favorite of mine throughout my childhood and, sadly, long since closed down. It had the additional charm of being located right next door to the city's only porno theater a few years before it too went out of business. Suffice it to say, this single block of the downtown area was both a place of taboo and treasure for me. And I felt the anticipation of both each time I walked down its sidewalk, wondering what I'd hear or see. But, like so many great places, it had to make way for the most aesthetically bankrupt and massively impersonal chain stores -- in this case, chain bookstores that serve more lattes and bottled water than actually great books that aren't mass marketed gimmicks or the result of some pop psych trend. Ephraim's was not such a place.

The minute you walked through the door, you were hit with the warm smell of old books -- a musty fragrance for which appreciation is no doubt on the decline in our digital culture. For me, it was the incense that prepared me for my weekly ritual of visiting this shop commonly overlooked by many citizens -- a place some might call a "hole in the wall" but one I found to be incredibly evocative and a genuine part of my cherished childhood memories. The man behind the counter (perhaps, Mr. Ephraim himself?) was as ancient as he was suspicious, and always kept an eye out for shoplifters in his poorly-lit store. But, I was a familiar face, having bought numerous books on mystery, suspense, and horror from him, so I was relieved of his scrutiny and given the usual nod of acknowledgment.

I was 15 and looking for something unusual to read when I

passed through the Occult section. (Back then, bookstores weren't relegating such books to the more pleasantly sounding "New Age" section.) The usual suspects were there: Crowley, Regardie, Summers, Lévi, Wheatley, Fortune, etc. I had read them all and found them terribly similar in many respects to the spiritual religions they often implied or claimed to distance themselves from. If they weren't calling forth the names of angels or devils (did it even matter which?) into protective circles, it was the usual warmed-over Christianity that didn't smell or taste any better with a new coating slathered on it. So, I was pretty much expecting the standard fare in this particular section when my eyes stopped upon a pair of books -- one black, one reddish-purple -- wedged tightly in between sinister tomes of astrology, telekinesis, and reincarnation. Fittingly enough, I went with the book on the left first.

Right away, it was apparent that this was a book that wasn't trying to hide its intentions or straddle any sort of ideological fence. The bold simplicity of its cover design and book title alone let me know that this was going to be very different from its shelfmates. I had read another one of the author's books, *The Compleat Witch*, in 1981, but I knew there was more to the story. So, I purchased *The Satanic Bible*, along with its then-magenta covered companion, *The Satanic Rituals*, and took the bus home, certain that these were to be memorable reads.

As I would discover while reading both books in teenage secrecy, this was definitely not what I might call "all feathers and no meat." In fact, TSB was much more than just a provocative title: it contained an actual philosophy based upon the reality of carnal existence and living one's life to its fullest. It rightfully championed mankind as being above his self-created gods and, as such, being totally responsible for his successes and failures. Like the mythological Lucifer's transformation into the autonomous Satan, man's penchant for exploration, independence, and drive shouldn't be caged but, rather, exercised and applauded. Anton LaVey's book made that very proclamation by invoking mythology's most relatable archetype and, like Milton and Twain before him, further proving just how much the characterization of the Devil -- as accuser, iconoclast, questioner -- is a positive and integral part of the human animal.

I was also pleasantly surprised to learn that Satanism rejects the entire concept of spirituality -- no ifs, ands, or buts. This isn't a religion that commands you to pray to an externalized god or to become one with the goddess. Satanism is a carnal religion which celebrates man's animal nature, abandoning any belief in or worship of an anthropomorphic being or deity. Rather than prostrating to some imaginary cosmic babysitter, Satanism upholds the self as a god, though obviously not an omniscient and all-powerful one. What godhood means to us is that we are the center of our universes, and we are wholly accountable for our actions. Our standpoint is that there is no Heaven or Hell, no literal gods or devils, no divinity, no bad juju, no sacred truths, no karma -- just us. If there is anything to fear about Satanists, it should be our advocacy of total responsibility, our support of unfettered justice, and our repudiation of all spiritual beliefs -- concepts most people are either too scared or too weak to embrace.

And it made all the more sense to me that those aligned with Satanism are in the minority, especially since one cannot "try" to be one. Indoctrination is for the masses, the hoi polloi, the Great Unwashed, and they seem well suited for it. The majority of any civilization will forever be held sway by popular sentiment, as a means to "fit in" or appear "just like the rest." We as Satanists have known from our earliest years that we are a breed apart. We know we are born and not made. We find great pride in our individuality, great joy in our solitary pursuits, and great incompatibility with the mindless and unprofitable conformity of those whom Nietzsche calls "the many too many." We are wolves among sheep.

Even before discovering Satanism, or even knowing there was a name for it, I intuitively understood it as a reality of my individual existence. As a child, I was all too reminded that I was far more intelligent and developmentally advanced than my so-called peers. Although I naturally fell into a leadership role in the rare event I was in a group setting, I generally preferred to play by myself: inventing my own worlds, creating all sorts of media, reading "grown-up" books, and truly enjoying my own company. Looking out the castle window, I found most of the children my age to be tedious little drones with no fire, no spark, no imagination. And I unashamedly used myself as the comparison: "Why couldn't they be more like me," rather than, "Why can't I be more like them?" The latter is acceptable. The former, heresy.

As a youngster, I also gravitated to the dark side of entertainment. While kids my age ran around their backyards pretending to be Luke Skywalker or Princess Leia, I was amassing my Imperial army from a box filled with Stormtrooper figures to crush "the rebel scum." Nightly, children around the neighborhood were being read tales of Snow White and Sleeping Beauty, while I was reading tales of mystery and the macabre in novels, comic books, and magazines. They were watching *Romper Room* and *Sesame Street*. I was watching *The Addams Family*, *The Twilight Zone*, and virtually every movie with Vincent Price, Christopher Lee, and Peter Cushing airing every Saturday on *Creature Double Feature*. At every turn, my interests and fascinations seemed to not connect with theirs. And the most culturally blasphemous part is that I couldn't have cared less.

And because of my lack of concern for such disrelation, I could truly enjoy my amazing and highly unconventional upbringing. Having moved and traveled a great deal around the United States, I was introduced to an incredibly diverse spectrum of people, traversing regional differences, individual personalities, lifestyle orientations, economic levels, and multitudinous views on life. It was a grand adventure and a solid education on the human condition -- one I didn't have to learn the hard way. I wasn't browbeaten for expressing my own opinions and my own way of seeing the world -- quite the opposite, actually. I was allowed to be creative and inspired and, when desired, I gained my moments of solitude without being harped on or made to feel bad. I was encouraged at all times to be both open-minded and critically thinking. I was exposed to many forms of cultural expression through my pre-teen years: music (chiefly, classical), literature, art, theater, and the social sciences -- the last, from an unending collection of books that lined the walls of my home. I was given a wealth of love, intellectual guidance, openness, respect, and attention from my mother. As a man nearing middle age, I couldn't say enough regarding just how proud of her I am, and how proud I am to be her son. When I see so many dishonest and jaded parent-child relationships in the world, I consider myself immeasurably fortunate.

My teen years were spent smack dab in the middle of the Reagan Era and during the rise of what would later be known as "Satanic Panic" -- a period of time marked by media-fueled hysteria against Satanists, replete with false accusations of child molestation, rape, and murder. Had I been an adult at the time of its onset, with a career and a family to worry about, it might have been a dangerous time to be an "out" Satanist in some areas of the United States -- not because I was doing something "wrong" but because the overblown falsehoods had escalated into a 20th century witch-hunt. Fortunately, I wasn't an adult. I was a teenager enjoying with impunity the fruits of individuation and rebellion that are the hallmarks of adolescence. And, yes, with a pentagram necklace around my neck.

Satanic Panic got into full swing about midway through high school for me. Before that, an obscene number of my fellow students thought my pentagram was a Star of David and that I was a Jew, which was funny then and even funnier now. When all of the tacky TV talk shows started giving attention to the lies and misinformation, that naiveté turned to fear and I was avoided like the plague -- advantageous for me, the budding misanthrope. For what seemed like forever, the powerless and the stupid were scrambling onto the stages of *Geraldo*, *Donahue*, *Sally Jessy Raphael*, *Montel* and many others, claiming to be "occult experts" or "survivors," having no idea what Satanism really is, appearing to really believe their own nonsense, and here was this 16 year old kid who knew better -- infinitely better than all of the "concerned" parents, druggie metal kids, deluded clergy, robotic audience members, instigating show hosts, and then actual news journalists parroting what daytime talk television was clearly feeding them. Through all of that time, I often felt like the sane person locked in the asylum along with the lunatics. It was, without doubt, a front row education in mob mentality.

Of course, I would be remiss if I didn't mention the flirtation with Satanism common amongst the fanbase of heavy metal in the 1980s. Because it was definitely there. Except that the metal majority's attraction to it was built upon very Christian assumptions of what Satanism is, thanks to not only the abovementioned talk shows, but all of the Christian literature that erroneously painted us in destructive and criminal tones. In other words, not Satanism. In part a reaction to such Christian-fed propaganda, album covers sporting pentagrams and lyrics bellowing for the conjuration of Satan himself were *de rigueur* and routinely expected by the genre's devotees. As a fan of '80s metal (and not necessarily of its fans), I witnessed firsthand the glaring misinterpretation of my religion by loser drug addicts and music subculture drones commonplace in any local "scene." Most of the time, this interest in Satanism was of the "shock the parents" variety and in the slim minority of cases, merely musically-contrived devil worship poorly masquerading as genuine Satanism. You even see some of that today amongst the new breed of extreme music. And still most of them have probably never read *The Satanic Bible* (let alone critically), and a fair number of them would no doubt fail to meet Satanism's standards. I can assure you that substance abuse, vandalism, and lack of direction in life don't cut it -- a sentiment clearly reflected in even our basic literature.

Satanic Panic ended right around my mid-20s, which is also when the World Wide Web went public (approx. 1993). With the lies of "Satanic ritual abuse" and "occult conspiracy" nicely discredited by the Federal Bureau of Investigation, the real facts about Satanism could get to people through the continued online presence of Church of Satan media representatives and their relaying of info on their sites. And I've definitely seen the entire evolution of Satanism on the Internet, right from the very beginning. I've been online since May of 1984 when I signed up with my first ISP, CompuServe. I began posting information on Satanism to that service as far back as 1987, then on America Online and various newsgroups throughout the 1990s, and then in 1997, I launched Purging Talon's web presence to promote my various media products under that name, first started in the offline world back in 1993. More on my media company can be found in the "composite interview" located in the Appendix of this book.

And although the Internet has made accurate information on Satanism a lot easier to find (as well as bogus miscellanea from folks who come and go in the blink of an eye), I have to recall how it was before everyone was plugged into the online world. When I discovered Dr. LaVey's books in the 1980s, I knew of no one else like me. Moreover, I didn't require others like me. If you had questioned me on that during my teens, I would have told you that it was just me and a book, and that's all it needed to be. I didn't need webpages, online CoS reps, and downloadable files to exhaustively explain or clarify Satanism to me. One book did that job quite proficiently, and I got it right off the bat. And if Dr. LaVey and I had been the only Satanists on the planet, I was thoroughly comfortable with that as well. I think that's a pretty healthy attitude, one I don't always see in younger folks who might obsessively pore over the posts of a popular Satanic message board or who send me a deluge of inquiring e-mails, looking for a pat on the back or to pick the brains of their betters. I sometimes see a lot of desperate "identity" placed into these online personae, perhaps at the expense of actually going out and enjoying one's life. And while I certainly find some merit in limited online communication, it is no substitute for the real world and all of its pleasures.

And that's what Satanism is all about: the real world. Not a world constructed upon wishful platitudes and unsubstantiated promises of life after death, but a very tangible place of potential for those who possess the intellect and the instinct to achieve excellence and happiness in their lives -- here and now! The real world doesn't care about prayers or excuses or empty posturing. Those are for people trying to escape the real world in the form of whatever type of "running away" from reality they feel is required. As a Satanist, I have no use for such fantasy living. The "great indulgence" of life compels me, not trudging through a dreary and deprived existence in anticipation of dying and then presumedly moving onto a realm whose actuality is more than highly suspect. Such denial and naiveté are fit for slaves. Not me.

I bear the Devil's mark. That is, I reject all anti-life doctrines which seek to rob people of their basic intelligence, their potential success, and their precious time. And that sharply distinguishes a person from the mass of human sheep content with allowing their lives to be orchestrated by those other than themselves. Far from being a mark of shame, bearing such "undefiled wisdom" is a mark of pride and progress which truly separates the wheat from the chaff. It is my hope that the following essays illustrate that very fact in greater depth for the reader. Perhaps, you might even learn something.

Most of the material in this book was published between 1993-2007 in either *Not Like Most* magazine or the long-defunct *Poo Poo Magazine*, both publications released by Purging Talon. Some of these essays have been reworked, updated, and otherwise improved upon in various ways from their original versions, which might be of particular interest to longtime fans of NLM. The remainder of material was previously unpublished and appears here for the first time. I would also invite you to the Appendix of this book for additional discourse, which might enhance your understanding of this work and of Satanism in general.

It should also be mentioned that this is not a strict primer on Satanism. Though, comprehending the material herein will not require that you have an extensive grasp on Satanic philosophy, either. Wherever possible, I have attempted to further explain concepts that might be more familiar to Satanists, but to get the most out of this book and to gain a greater understanding of terms such as Psychic Vampire, Lesser Magic, Lex Talionis, The Balance Factor, and more, I would highly suggest you peruse many of the online documents posted to churchofsatan.com and, even before that, read *The Satanic Bible*. Any education on Satanism starts with that book, and not this one.

Stumbling upon *The Satanic Bible* in my mid-teens was serendipity with a capital "S." I could have easily bought a book by H.P. Lovecraft or Agatha Christie that chilly night at Ephraim's and simply not spotted TSB in the process. But I did. And I am eternally grateful for all of the brilliance and insight Dr. LaVey brought to all of us. Without Anton Szandor LaVey, this book you are now holding would not exist. Neither would Satanism -- a fact no doubt troubling to religious fanatics and rabid pseudo-Satanists alike. So, it is with great pride that I put this collection into the world and dedicate it to Dr. LaVey, the church he built, and the legacy he leaves behind. Ever forward!

Magister Matt G. Paradise
Halloween XLII A.S. (2007)

Bearing The Devil's Mark

FURTHER EVIDENCE OF THE SATANIC AGE

June 6th, 2006. Los Angeles. The Decompression commences with the lighting of black candles and the ringing of the bell. Faint undertones of snarling beasts and ominous winds are barely discernible. In the dark distance, a giant trapezoidal structure emerges, supporting the supine form of a nude woman and flanked by towers of maddening angles. High above, the Sigil of Baphomet comes into view, as if to scan the congregants with its penetrating stare. A fog begins to fill the hall. In the fore, a podium lit by a single spotlight from above stands waiting. As ambient sounds echo throughout, the Priest enters the illuminated space and approaches the platform. With thunder in his voice, he opens the ritual...

"In nomine Dei nostri Satanas Luciferi excelsi!"

And so began the Satanic High Mass, performed at the Center For Inquiry West with over 100 Satanists from around the globe, the largest Satanic ritual in recorded history. And indeed it was history. Not only did its size and media attention make it noteworthy, but it also marked the 40th year of existence for the first religious organization to defy convention and proudly take up the name of the Devil himself -- the Church of Satan.

For those fortunate enough to have gained entrance to this exclusive event, the energy that night will be remembered as undeniable and inspiring. As an audience participant, I witnessed a production so immersive -- in terms of stark visuals, atmospheric music, and dramatic dialogue -- that I couldn't tell you how much time had passed at all. After the Mass, I remember taking a moment to look around at this small sampling of our meta-tribe, truly realizing the impact that Anton Szandor

LaVey and his *Satanic Bible* have had, not only on me but on so many others: past, present and, no doubt, future. And such a wide variance of age was represented that night. I spotted four generations present in the theater hall, further testament to the rootedness and longevity of the Satanic philosophy.

At one point during the festivities, I felt almost pulled back in time to the feelings of discovery I had in the early-1980s when I first opened the book that would alter my life forever, giving me a rather controversial but fitting name for who and what I've always been: Satanist. I thought a lot about how many years had passed since I aligned myself with the world's most feared religion. I thought about what it must have been like in the early years of the organization, the very significant outgrowth of those years into the present day, and the many years there are to look forward to. We've come a long way... and we've only just begun.

Of course, our detractors of the past would paint a different picture, if many of them were even slightly relevant today or even around anymore. As any organization of note receives, we've had numerous predictions of our demise over the years, a few lies to the effect that the Church of Satan closed its figurative doors (over and over again, apparently), and an assortment of very transparent namecalling, griping, projection, and sour grapes from those who'd like to see us go away but will remain eternally disappointed. Yes, we've outlasted all of them, proving without a doubt that we were much more important to them and their frail egos than they could have possibly mattered to us, be they bible thumpers or disgruntled ex-CoS members -- often one and the same, depending on when you catch them.

But what's happened in the world since the Church of Satan was formed in 1966 that's truly important? What changes in the way people think, feel, and behave have occurred that reflect a shift towards the carnal (read: earthly) and away from the spiritual? How far has this shift gone? And are the gods of the recent past being abandoned in favor of more rational and life-affirming values? To answer these questions, one needn't look further than upon the timeline of what has transpired between then and now.

The 1960s

San Francisco brought the world a great many things. Jack London and

Robert Frost were born there. Wells Fargo was founded in SF during the Gold Rush. It's where convicted crime boss Al Capone spent his remaining days behind the walls of the island prison known as Alcatraz. And "the City by the Bay" had also become the main center of activity for the Beat Generation, homosexual rights, and hippies. But on the 30th of April 1966, a new movement in San Francisco would arise and spread itself across a world which would both embrace and revile it. The movement began on that Walpurgis Eve with the founding of the Church of Satan.

And although the Church of Satan came out of the same era and geographical location as the hippie movement, the similarities largely stop there. Satanism eschewed and condemned the hippie lifestyle on many levels: chief amongst them were the unrealistic belief in world peace, the ludicrous assertion of a communal "free" system, the contempt for law and order, and the counterproductive use and abuse of illegal drugs. Satanism promotes rational self-interest, productive pride, and responsible (read: pragmatic) behavior, qualifiers lacking in the recklessly unrestrained practices of the flower children. And it is these qualifiers that are key to understanding the broad separation between what they were about and what Satanism has always represented.

And as the law of cause and effect so often comes into play, it would be this unchecked and irrational hedonism that would serve as the hippie downfall, concluding in mass homelessness, drug-induced psychoses, rape, forced prostitution, narcotic addiction, and the list goes on. Not exactly "peace and love" and certainly nothing to be admired or glorified.

Though, what is probably more obvious to Satanists than to most other folks is that the hippie movement and Christianity share a great deal of philosophy, aspects of a parallel mindset that are wholly incompatible with Satanism. Both posit the not-so-golden rule: do unto others as you would have them do unto you. Both vainly preach the unconditional love for total strangers. Both require a self-imposed adversary to combat in order to maintain identity and purpose -- Christianity needs "Satan," hippies need "the system." Both compiled a hodge podge of previous mystical traditions and backwoods folklore that ultimately caused more harm than good. Conversely, Satanism smashed through all of the holy writs and desperate countercultural values with a solid philosophy based firmly on the human animal and the physical world in which we live, a framework forged in reality and not in myopia and flowery idealism.

Probably the only commonalities Satanism had with the hippie movement were the concepts of sexual exploration and the questioning of your environment. But, unlike the renegade peaceniks, Satanists knew to avoid projecting pipe dreams and reckless abandon into the mix, keeping well in mind that the Balance Factor applies to all arenas of human exploit.

This is why Satanism is not, nor could ever be, a "do whatever you want" philosophy. Again, cause and effect is immutable and not recognizing this law of nature is oftentimes a recipe for disaster and a failure in Lesser Magic.

The 1970s

Hot on the heels of the self-proclaimed "love generation" came the Swinging '70s. By this time, indulgence was rolling full-steam ahead thanks in part to increased acceptance of human sexuality but also the availability of oral contraceptives for unmarried women in 1972 and the legalization of abortion in 1973 (*Roe v. Wade*). Now that both single men and women could engage in relatively-protected sex, the stage was set for the rise and popularity of swingers clubs, strip joints, wife swapping, group sex, and a then-ambiguous love for pornography -- material which is far more explicit in this decade than ever before. For whatever personal reasons many may have had for this type of exploration, it's apparent that the exploration is not only happening, but at a less and less shameful rate.

And that lack of inhibition didn't stay behind closed doors. In the early-1970s, the outpouring of acceptability for "dirty movies" was captured during a period of "porno chic" which showed that it was quite hip to indulge in viewing pornographic films, even in mainstream moviehouses. Major celebrities such as Johnny Carson, Jack Nicholson, and Truman Capote checked out *Deep Throat* when it hit the theaters in 1972 and porn stars such as Marilyn Chambers, Harry Reems, and Linda Lovelace were practically household names. Given permission by its own culture, many of the herd in America could now explore their animal nature in the bedroom and discuss it socially, paving the way for more mindful acceptance later on. The Devil in Miss Jones, indeed.

It should also be noted that, until 1988, it was a crime to produce or perform in an adult film (under pandering and prostitution laws), though viewing these same films, according to the Presidential Commission on Obscenity and Pornography in 1970, was quite acceptable. The Commission also stated that not only does porn not lead to delinquent or criminal behavior as previously thought, but that, reflecting further back to a 1969 Supreme Court decision (*Stanley v. Georgia*, 394 U.S. 557), it's also something that people could view in the privacy of their own homes. Today, the idea of legally prosecuting or punishing mainstream porn stars and the companies who make and sell their movies seems positively Victorian, if not Medieval, and certainly a very much failed chapter in Christian moral history. Just log onto the Internet for indisputable proof of that failure.

In so many ways, the 1970s saw the genesis, if you will, of people casting off the vestiges of Christian guilt and living life free of such impersonal social commandments, just as Dr. LaVey had predicted.

And speaking of the good Doctor, his presence was in many places during the late-1960s and the 1970s, including the mainstream press (*Time*, *Newsweek*, *Look*, *McCalls*), and television (*Phil Donahue*, *The Tonight Show*, *Joe Pyne*). Satanic symbolism and philosophy were no longer scattered through the pages of dusty books or whispered nervously in hushed tones, but alive and flowing freely through conventional culture, finding a voice within the advancement of social and sexual attitudes in this decade. This isn't a silent cardboard cutout of a funny red figure with a pitchfork and a pointed tail, but a Devil that actually talks back, and now one which is being increasingly listened to. And watched.

The Devil was also the main feature of many movies in the 1970s. In fact, a notable onslaught of Satan-centered cinema enters the theaters through this decade, riding on the coattails of *Rosemary's Baby* (1968) and the publicity of the Church of Satan, including *The Exorcist*, *The Omen*, *Damien: Omen II*, *To The Devil A Daughter*, *The Tempter*, *Race With The Devil*, *Satan's Cheerleaders*, *Alucarda*, *The Devil's Rain*, *The Satanic Rites of Dracula*, *Mephisto Waltz*, *The Brotherhood of Satan*, *Satan's Blood*, *Don't Deliver Us From Evil*, *Asylum of Satan*, *Satan's Children*, *Dr. Dracula*, and *In Lust For A Vampire*, to provide but a meager sampling. Now, certainly, these films rarely if at all accurately represent Satanism (seeing as they are works of fiction and they are sensationalized by Hollywood), but that's not their job. Their job is to entertain, but they also inadvertently provoked curiosity in actual Satanism, proving once more that people come to us from the unlikeliest of places.

Whether through the Big Screen or mainstream media coverage or in-house publications, Satan was well in the public spotlight during the '70s, hand in hand with the radical cultural changes of the time. But, like any maturation period, there are bound to be some growing pains and it is the following decade during which we hear the sounds of such discomfort and denial the loudest.

The 1980s

With the start of the Reagan Era (1980-1988) came a wave of social and political conservatism, deeply founded in strict Christian morality. From this, the rise of the Christian Right came in the form of leaders such as Pat Robertson and Jerry Falwell -- individuals who helped mobilized Christian voters to elect Ronald Reagan to the presidency based on mutual religio-political views. And within the first few years of Reagan's initial term in office, his Christian Right cronies and their ilk had begun to back a rather serious fabrication: that there existed a worldwide network of "Satanists" who were sacrificing people, breeding babies for ritual slaughter, kidnapping, brainwashing, and infiltrating all avenues of public life to spread its sinister influence over the planet. Christian therapists "found" that the alleged child abuse victims they had as clients might not have been merely abused but, additionally, were unwilling pawns in this giant conspiracy. Whether their projection is based upon mindless religious indoctrination or mindful manipulation of people for self gain, these therapists, through the use of their patients, created the hoax of Satanic Ritual Abuse (or SRA -- later, it would be referred to as "Satanic Panic," a retronym culled from the book of the same name by Jeffrey Victor, a leading exponent of debunking SRA).

This period of time would also prompt many representatives of the Church of Satan to appear in interviews and on talk shows such as *Donahue*, *Geraldo*, *Oprah Winfrey*, and *Sally Jessy Raphael* to give our side of the story. And although it might have had some impact, the well-fed automatons of the viewing audience were often too frightened by fabricated scare stories to even listen to the facts. (It is interesting to note that Geraldo Rivera completely recanted and apologized for his involvement in spreading the lie of SRA on a CNBC show in December of 1995, on which he was quoted as saying, "I want to announce publicly that [I was] a firm believer of the 'Believe The Children' movement of the 1980s, that started with the McMartin trials in California, but NOW I am convinced that I was terribly wrong... and many innocent people were convicted and went to prison as a result... AND I am equally positive [that the] 'Repressed Memory Therapy Movement' is also a bunch of CRAP...")

Also dragged onto the witch-hunt bandwagon was the assumed influence of heavy metal music upon the youth -- a purported gateway to Satanism, as espoused by such *de facto* Christian Right organizations as the Parents Music Resource Center, Focus On The Family, Back In Control, and Bob Larson Ministries. Indeed, many metal bands of the time dabbled in Satanic symbolism and dark lyrics, but the overwhelming majority of such usage was for shock purposes and definitely not rooted in legitimate Satanic philosophy. Evidence lending, it seems that the bulk of these musical acts, as well as their accusers, had never even read *The Satanic Bible*. No surprise there.

But given the misguidedness of the Christian Right, heavy metal ended up the scapegoat for maladjusted kids, teen suicides, and various delinquent acts. Court trials such as those that blamed the deaths of youngsters on metal music were a legal farce that only proved that blameshifting and lack of parental responsibility were not the fault of Ozzy Osbourne, Judas Priest, or any other artist, musical or otherwise. But, many people did indeed make money off of such controversy, including individuals who formed censorship groups, members of the Christian radio community, spouses of politicians, and lobbyists for the Christian Right. They certainly weren't following the purportedly altruistic example of their savior by doing it for free.

By the end of the 1980s, a lot of lessons were learned. A new level of skepticism was reached, traversing religion, politics, sexuality, economics, and the role of the media in our lives -- the very "questioning of all" that is encapsulated in the archetype (and very literal translation) of Satan. This would also be the last hurrah for fundamentalist Christianity as it said goodbye to its relative political clout and the effectiveness of its propaganda while it watched a culture much more interested in the real world (than an imaginary one in the sky) become progressively more aware of those who wish to chip away at our pluralistic society.

The 1990s

The early-1990s saw a vast awakening on many fronts -- most notable to

Satanists was the end of Satanic Panic, entirely debunked by the FBI as simply being nonexistent (*1992 FBI Report -- "Satanic Ritual Abuse"* by Kenneth V. Lanning, Supervisory Special Agent of the Behavioral Science Unit, National Center for the Analysis of Violent Crime). From there, local, state, and federal law enforcement agencies, being formerly hoodwinked by the Christian therapy movement that incited the delirium for its own ends, had now learned a valuable lesson in how not to react to hysteria and hearsay. The "victims" of this conspiratorial con job had also shown their disapproval by filing numerous lawsuits against these same Christian therapists to the tune of rather large settlements. The disinformation machine started in the 1980s to slander and scapegoat Satanists (and anyone fundamentalist Christians incompetently deemed a "Satanist") came to a grinding halt in the early-'90s, all to be dismantled and jettisoned for the demented fairy tale that it was.

What also came of this was a widespread awareness of how the Christian Right and their allies, once considered great moral arbiters by the more delusional of the herd, were simply opportunistic religionists with the aim of subjugating dissenters and installing a theocratic political system in the United States. These people didn't just want to have their cake and eat it, too -- they wanted to own the entire bakery! But, like the invalidation of Satanic Panic, greater numbers of people in the 1990s were seeing these modern snake oil salesmen for what they are, and gaining yet another example of the excesses of the God religions pushing themselves upon a secular world. These days, such religious "kooks" are fodder for the routines of such rational and beloved comedians as George Carlin, Penn & Teller, Louis Black, and David Cross -- funnymen whose rather unfavorable views towards much of the God religions are responded to with copious applause, worldwide popularity, and impressive album sales. They truly do the Devil's work.

Regarding Christianity as a whole in the 1990s, no other controversy surrounding this dead mythology could possibly compete in modern times with the Roman Catholic sex abuse scandal. It should be no secret that sexual repression as an end product of mandatory celibacy starting in seminary and extending through the life of a priest might actually surface as pedophilia. In more exact terms, when someone's sexuality is interrupted and halted at an early age and then not allowed to mature and express itself in a healthy and consensual manner (let alone ANY manner), it sometimes manifests in rather inappropriate ways later in life. Basically, they pick up at the age in which they left off.

Such seems the case with many if not all of the convicted priests. And let's not fool ourselves here. This aberrant outcome is the direct result of Christianity and other religions that attempt to control, circumvent, and suppress sexuality, especially when you add in the condemnation of homosexuality, if same-sex desire is applicable. Though, it is also the responsibility of these priests to physically remove themselves from such archaic repression -- at the very least, to avoid recidivism -- and seek out therapy if needed. Free will dictates that they are to blame for their complicity, and they should receive no lenience in sentencing simply because they are "men of the cloth." (An excellence documentary, one of many on the subject of exposing pedophile priests and the concealment of the entire issue by the Catholic Church, is the 2006 release of *Deliver Us From Evil*, directed by Amy Berg.)

While the Christian religious community deals with irrepressible scandals and a steady decline in popularity, carnal pursuits are gaining ground exponentially and proving to be far more enjoyable and stimulating than unrealistic behavioral demands and contradicting Bible parables.

Pornography, once hypocritically shunned and persecuted by religious zealots in positions of power, has now gone mainstream as never before. What served as the catalyst, interestingly enough, was a simple visual media format. The introduction of the videocassette propelled the adult film industry in the 1980s, allowing otherwise sexually repressed people ("religious" or not) to enjoy adult entertainment in their own homes, thus avoiding the contrived shame that came with visiting porno theaters. And by the '90s, not only is the act of masturbation a more freely expressed topic among people, but the masses are given greater access to porn through the Internet, breaking down more walls of abstinence and guilt formerly gained from religious indoctrination. Even former and current porn stars are now a part of popular culture -- books, music videos, Hollywood films, album covers, gossip TV programs -- something unheard of decades back.

Of course, the Internet brings more into people's homes than just sexual entertainment. Amongst the cheap glitter of online distractions resides a wealth of very useful knowledge on a wide variety of subjects, including those of differing cultures, varying viewpoints, and, yes, even Satanism. In addition to the official Church of Satan website (www.churchofsatan.com), a number of CoS member sites have sprung up alongside the Information Superhighway, pointing those who are curious about Satanism -- for self-education or practical application -- towards credible info and what many of the Church of Satan's most creative and productive members are up to. Likewise, the purchase of our books through online sellers has made acquiring our hard copy texts practically effortless. Like those who felt self-conscious about being seen outside of porn theaters or adult "bookstores," people from around the world can educate themselves at CoS-approved sites and order our books away from prying eyes. They certainly aren't able to be frightened by their religious communities to avoid the facts on Satanism these days, thanks to a very carnal endeavor: technology.

With the global use of such advanced technology, it is far too apparent that Satanism is the genie that cannot be conveniently stuffed back into the bottle, and the less braindead members of the God religions know it, too. They just wish that you didn't know it.

The 2000s

If there was one event during this decade that so glaringly illustrated the insanity of God-religious fundamentalism, it is the one which began at 8:46 a.m. EST on the 11th of September 2001.

Four commercial U.S. airliners were hijacked by Islamic terrorists: two were flown into the World Trade Center towers, one into the Pentagon, and the last crashed in rural Pennsylvania. It would later be discovered that the wanton deaths of 3000 people were the result of a *fatwa* issued in 1998 by al-Qaeda leader, Osama bin Laden, and for some very religious reasons.

Like Christianity, Islam is steeped in rhetoric hostile to nonbelievers, calling for punishments including torture and death. Both the *Holy Bible* and the *Koran* are so packed full of hatred and bloodshed towards "blasphemers", "heretics," and "infidels" (not to mention women and homosexuals) that the parallels are irrefutable. The fact that Christianity has ceased to continue this part of its history in modern day (that is, excluding abortion clinic bombers and apocalyptic Christian cult leaders) while certain Islamic followers act it out is all a matter of time and circumstance. They are cut from the same religionist cloth no matter how much softsoaping and backpedaling their respective spin doctors apply. The difference between back then and now is that more and more people are paying attention to the spiritual shell game being played and mindfully walking away from the mess.

And while many thought about greater security at U.S. Customs checkpoints following 9/11, many others thought about the unflattering but valid implications behind this religiously-supported act and how dangerous to civilization such agents of imaginary deities are. By a shared Abrahamic doctrine, the true believers are purportedly above the laws of man (which they believe to be secondary to the laws of their God), they do not care for human life (including their own, as it is only transitory to them in their quest for Heaven), and all who disagree with them are expendable. Same idea behind the Holy Crusades, the Salem Witch Trials, jihads, and various religious "cleansings" around the world. They are all inextricably bound to a legacy of human repression, rampant censorship, the stunting of scientific progress, and millions upon millions of people slaughtered in the name of a fiction.

From same-sex marriage to digital rights management, attitudes were changing in step with a more educated and tech-savvy culture -- one that has no need for faith-based hearsay or empty promises. As a result of these well evident changes, the legal system would have to evolve and adapt in kind. In some instances, the system has done just that.

Anyone remember Roy Moore? Moore was the Alabama Chief Justice who, in 2001, decided all on his own to have a 5,300-pound monument bearing the Ten Commandments installed in the rotunda of the judicial building in which he held court, and without consulting any of his colleagues. This was also after receiving sizable criticism for hanging a wooden plaque of the Commandments in his courtroom and requiring pre-session prayers. In August of 2003, a U.S. District Judge ordered that Moore remove the monument, which Moore adamantly refused and was summarily charged with ethics violations. One week later, a federal order was granted and the monument was removed. In November of that same year, Chief Justice Moore was removed from office by a unanimous decision of the Court of the Judiciary, in effect recognizing how unconstitutional Moore's flagrant endorsement of Christianity was. If this had happened 20 years earlier, Moore would have probably gotten to keep his religious eyesore and Reagan would have no doubt exonerated him. Oh, how times have changed.

But, for some, it's the same ol' song and dance. And someone who definitely paid the piper was Ted Haggard. This former evangelical preacher, a founder of the Association of Life-Giving Churches, and former leader of the National Association of Evangelicals was a staunch anti-gay marriage advocate. The same man *Time* magazine listed as one of the top 25 most influential evangelicals in America had traveled extensively, delivering his homophobic sermons through television, film, and live appearances. Fans of Haggard knew him as a model of good Christian living and an all-around straight shooter. What his congregation didn't know was that, for a three-year period, Haggard was secretly having regular sexual encounters with a former male prostitute. The scandal hit the presses in late-2006 and we were all once more entertained by yet another self-contradicting servant of the lord in the spirit of Jim Bakker and Jimmy Swaggart. Good thing all of these men had a more sexually-relaxed culture to answer to. Oh, the irony.

But it does make one ponder the promising extent to which sexual views have advanced in our culture. Once upon a time in our not-too-distant past, it was a crime to have non-procreative sex, straight or gay, and lengthy terms of imprisonment were a potential outcome before the mid-1960s. Now with the abolition of all U.S. sodomy laws as of June 2003, that is no longer a concern. Of course, it is hardly a secret that sodomy laws came about in the first place as the result of religious (notably, Christian) dictates. The name itself comes from Sodom, the city purportedly destroyed by the Judeo-Christian god "by brimstone and fire" in retaliation for its so-called spiritual defiance. And the motives for these sodomy laws were in direct alignment with the Christian agenda: sodomy doesn't result in offspring ("be fruitful and multiply"), it is more heavily relied upon by homosexuals (who are an "abomination" in the eyes of their fictional Jehovah), it encourages masturbation (the sin of Onan), and muzzling a fearful population into compliance, as history has taught us, starts with the repression/control of sexuality -- particularly, sex that does not support or forward the "divine plan" of the dominant religion.

What is certainly not part of any divine plan, but was inevitable all the same, is the rising tide of atheism amongst the young and the not-so-young in current Western culture. By and large, our youth no longer exist in a well-regulated bubble of parental lockdown from all matters of the outside world but now have a much more realistic and well-rounded perspective on that same world as it is, and not as their elders think it "ought to be." Some of this comes from popular and not-so-popular culture introducing a less veneered view of life, such as it might come from music, independent media, and certainly the Internet. Given a more inclusive education on the human condition, young people today can cast aside irrational, inaccurate, and speculative belief systems in favor of more concrete, provable and practical knowledge. And they are definitely learning about us.

Even within youth culture, we've seen a very visible welcoming of devil-themed attire, tattoos, jewelry, and various other means by which to indulge in our symbolism. Everywhere you look, it seems that adolescents (and definitely older folks, too) are flashing the Sign of the Horns -- a religious hand gesture formerly popularized by heavy metal, but directly acquired from us before then. (This hand gesture's casual usage has also prompted a great many people's curiosity to actually learn about Satanism. Funny how that works out.) Our own Magister Coop has stamped his devil artwork on everything from lunch boxes to playing cards, and there seems no end to the consumption of his creations. An entire sub-genre of metal music -- namely, black metal -- has formulated a staple image out of Satanic iconography and quasi-related lyrical themes. Some even owe their careers to it. And who could forget the tidal wave of media created by Church of Satan members that started as an upsurge in the 1990s but has become a literal Renaissance in the 21st century: books, magazines, works of art, photography, movies, documentaries, DVD video programs, music albums, TV shows, radio shows, podcasts, and more, much of which available from major retailers and various online sources.

When Dr. LaVey wrote that Christianity would die of its own obsolescence, it's evident that such "generational extinction" is heralded by the youth who've come of age in the post-1966 period since the Church of Satan's formation. No matter their affiliation, their godless numbers are increasing and it is pure music to the ears of any rational human being.

But, let's not whitewash these facts by dismissing the position of many of these pre-adults as mere teenage whim or fad. They have much older contemporaries as well, currently gathered under the media moniker of "the New Atheists." Authors such as Richard Dawkins, Sam Harris, Christopher Hitchens, Michael Martin, R.A. Sharpe, Victor Stenger, and many more in the late-20th and early-21st centuries are of an unapologetic breed. They are not taking the defensive position or excusing themselves for their remarks but are attacking the infantile need for a belief in a deity as outmoded, unnecessary, and in many cases, harmful to individuals and cultures at large. They pick up where such luminaries as Feuerbach, Schopenhauer and Nietzsche leave off and I would certainly recommend perusing their works as well.

The crumbling façade of God is falling fast, rapidly being replaced with towering testaments to rationality, critical thinking, personal responsibility, healthy ego expression, and human potential unhampered by ancient desert cult ethics. And as this "infernal empire" grows, so too will mankind's reach for facts over privileged lies, pleasure over abstinence, and life over religiously-induced obsessions with death. Even as sects of Christianity desperately attempt revisionism to seem more palatable to the masses (something Dr. LaVey foresaw in the 1960s), it is too little, too late. They are on an inevitable course towards eliminating so much of what is Christian about their framework and reaching the destination point of pure secularity.

Even some of the most fundamental Christian doctrine, much of which centuries old, has been miraculously canceled or reshaped by the various Christian churches in their last-ditch attempts to remain current and keep people in the pews. Gays and lesbians can now embrace the religion that, for centuries, actively sought to torture and murder them *en masse*. Filtered through the lens of "Queer Theology," Christianity is now refocused by the Metropolitan Community Church as a means to cherry-pick their way through the Bible (standard practice throughout the countless flavors of modern Christianity), as well as permitting those of either gender to hold the highest offices. In 2007, Pope Benedict XVI stated that there is substantial and valid scientific proof for the theory of evolution -- a statement that, had it been publicly spoken by any one of his historic predecessors, would have brought forth charges of blasphemy, often punishable by death. Concepts such as Hell and the Devil are now thought to be figurative rather than literal by many Christian denominations. In fact, a lot of what was once considered "the gospel truth" by Christians is now conveniently retagged as "metaphorical", "allegorical," or "symbolic" -- surprisingly from such folks as evangelist Billy Graham ("spiritual advisor" to several U.S. presidents) and the late Pope John Paul II. After all, it's a bit tough to push the whole rising from the dead spiel these days without sounding like a zombie movie. And I'm definitely not the only one to cheekily wonder how Noah acquired polar bears and penguins in the Middle East. And what to do with the seemingly narcotic-inspired Book of Revelation? Apparently, chucking the inconvenient parts is the order of the day.

Along similar revisionist lines, we have the Christian Atheists mentioned in *The Satanic Bible*, but now also Humanistic (or Atheistic) Jews, Cultural Mormons, and Secular Muslims -- perhaps comprised of people desperate to hang onto their childhood religious programming in the wake of intellectual maturity that stands to eliminate it. There are plenty of people who simply do not want to let go of their spiritual security blankets even after their otherwise mindful rejection of traditional religion, and we've seen prime examples of this within the alternative religious trends of New Age and Wicca -- both of which adhering to very god-religious precepts, but without the dreaded "G" word or many of the outdated social and political demands. Given the nature of these substitutes, it would appear that their unintended purpose is to wean those attracted to such revisionism off the teat of theism in preparation for secular life.

Sometimes, secularization occurs without any real effort, or simply by inaction. Not long ago, Christmas was an observance of the birth, albeit a dubious one, of Christianity's namesake. Through some lockstep obligation, many people once trudged their way to church on Christmas morning to tolerate endless services comprised of hymnal dirges and monotone preaching... just to run home and get to the presents. And while a minority of American citizens (largely those in isolated, rural, and/or southern communities) still feel that burning desire to "keep Christ in Christmas," the rest of the world has little to no concern for a fictional composite of previous pagan myths known as "Jesus." Today's Christmas season cuts out all of that virgin birth nonsense and celebrates material gain, indulgences, and the joy experienced with kith and kin. The national economy skyrockets as retail sales climb higher and sooner each year, and with nary a glimpse of the little babe from Bethlehem. Champagne and holiday feasts have overridden communion and pointless prayers -- and as well they should. Of course, the ringleader of this yuletide *bacchanalia* is a marketing creation known as Santa. And we all know what that name is an anagram for.

It stands to reason that if all of the carnal fun was instantaneously taken away from Christmas revelers, and religiosity was the only thing put back in its place, the entire holiday would fade away without so much as a whimper. Take note, believers! Be happy that Christmas, in any form, is even still around. Because your creed is vanishing at an exponential rate.

Even empirical evidence supports the reality that, for the vast majority of people in the Western world (and you can throw in most of the nominal Christians as well), premarital sex is perfectly acceptable, women aren't merely viewed as babymakers and housekeepers anymore, religious persecution is no longer appropriate, prayers aren't mandatory in public schools, and blacks aren't assumed to be inferior as a byproduct of the curse of Ham (*Genesis 9:20-27* -- it took the Mormons until 1978 to ditch racist policies related to this divine "curse"). All of this happened within the timeframe of the Church of Satan's existence.

In *The Satanic Bible*, Dr, LaVey puts forth his evidence for what was then a new Satanic Age. Since 1966, Western culture has irrevocably steered into a highly Satanic direction, paving the way for future generations to pick up the Promethean torch of progress and carry it forward without the encumbrance of superstitious religions upon them. That direction is clearly represented in every scientific advancement, every healthy indulgence practiced, every question asked concerning the "whys and wherefores" of popular thought, and in the growing number of people who leave behind spiritual fictions in favor of being the captains of their own destinies.

The verdict is in! The Age of Satan is undeniably here! And its championing of the carnal is a mirror to the world, reminding all who look into it of their truest and inescapable nature.

EGO TRANSFERENCE AND THE HERD

From the moment that we are born, the dominant culture indiscriminately presumes its mark and subjects us all to a life paradigm far more insistent and with more intended enforcement than even the laws of the State. Though traveling in many forms, the indoctrination to externalize your ego -- instead of keeping it where it would primarily benefit the self -- is a prevalent force in modern culture. Most of the cultures in which we live seek to perpetuate unquestioned acquiescence to that which profits all but the individual. Put more specifically, the power struggle is engineered to pull sentiment, loyalty, and focus (often, in that order) towards external entities, either real or invented -- especially, the latter, as they're often easier to assign and control.

Much is why Satanism isn't a religion congruent with mass appeal. Since we prize our individual nature, we are resilient to this social virus. Our separate identities, if I may use the term, are based on how we each define ourselves *to* ourselves, and not upon acceptance or rejection from those on the outside. At best, alien elements are kept pragmatically in mind for either utilization or avoidance (and, in some cases, mockery). Given any current climate, we're not exactly a predictable demographic.

One avenue down which this externalization journeys is in matters of career, or work. The phrase, "you are what you do" becomes the all-too-obedient rally cry of the self-oppressed, giving the term, "occupation" a whole new meaning. Some corporations even put this misdirection to music, as is evident in internally-used slogans and company songs ("Horst Wessel Lied," move over). Don't bother expecting these types to spit out much more than "I am a [fill in the job title]" because the ego's been sold. Though, for others, employment identity simply isn't a satisfactory enslavement.

Enter politics, that one giant, tri-colored ticker tape parade of mass ego-consignment. No longer does your average prole have to be content with his or her lot in life. Somehow, assigning the self to the label of Democrat or Republican is identity enough, and they can stand by these faux-representations regardless of issues, candidate promises, or actual results. If they're waving the flag like a good patriot, all the better. Their chosen politicians, their flag, their adopted feeling of superiority based on their nation's position of world power -- all of these furnish a sense of cultural importance or wisdom; a semblance, being better than nothing for them.

However, for the man who doesn't even care to pretend that he's thinking (let alone for himself), there's the wonderful world of sports. Not necessarily participating in them, mind you, but reveling in the mindless glory of armchair spectatorship, which serves in some capacity as the male equivalent of soap operas. For many, the performance of their favorite sports team is obliquely perceived as an achievement of theirs -- and the memorized stats, scores, and other related data on teams and players can fill the fan with a laughable sense of erudition, discernment, and purpose (and it's certainly cheaper than college). Vicariously, they can live through those whose athletic ability, on its worst day, is vastly superior to the audience member's best. Just take a look at the disproportionate number of, say, wrestling fans who are noticeably ill-prepared in the self-defense department, either in ability or actual physical limitations. Unfazed, they still manage to syphon off some might or the feeling of strength from those who excel at something they never will.

And if the sports team hails from the nearest geographical location to the fans, then it's "their" team, and should be supported regardless of performance. After all, there *are* egos at stake here.

Many of these wannabe-jocks, as well as those not of the Superbowl ilk, also find an astonishing sense of externalized ego in their choice of automobile. Once merely a mode of transportation, the automobile is now able to service even the most broken down ego. The more they fix the vehicle up (but not fix themselves up, mind you), the more horsepower it has and detailing it receives, the more their egos can be transferred to something for which they can obtain praise. Just look at the telling names under which these mechanized beasts often proceed: Bronco, Explorer, Mustang, Avalanche, Blazer, Outback, and the list goes on. Plus, it's just plain easier to surrender the self over this way, and in this convenience-based culture, isn't minimal effort what it's all about?

But, not all find comfort in the rough and tumble world of manufactured machismo. For the more socially outcast who still strive to play a modified and lesser-accepted version of the same game, the well-oiled machine of music subculture provides promise to an ego just waiting to be leased to the highest bidder. Image again enters the picture -- in fact, it's practically everything! To the ambitious acolyte, a media-friendly (or unfriendly) array of hairstyles, clothing, jewelry, footwear, and more are available through which to assume someone else's life and accomplishment by proxy, not to mention said celebrity's fanbase of other adherents, who will provide group identity in place of that ego that is just too frail to stand alone (and although this collectivism is more pervasive within sports fandom, it's very much here as well). Likewise, this breed can also be found as garden variety groupies attached to those of high to hyped acclaim in film or on television.

Of course, where the externalizing of the ego plays front and center on this maddeningly twirling globe of ours is within the rank and file of the God religions. No more thorough and mindless submission of the ego is possible than by emptying it into the construct of a god. Like the little dog behind the big dog, they can bark social dictates, cast judgment, condemn practices, and feel powerful, all by placing the ultimate authority onto a fictional deity, thus alleviating the follower of any responsibility or accountability -- that which a healthy and superior ego could actually take full brunt. Since *The Satanic Bible* has an entire chapter on this entire process, I direct you to those well-written pages for self-education, if needed.

Probably the biggest reason for the herd to externalize their egos is that their egos simply have no comparable substance. Since they are largely out of touch with their animal nature and so senselessly locked into social assimilation to a disposable culture, an otherwise natural process of self-fulfillment has been inverted to save the person from too much self-examination and self-realization. Consider it an elaborate and life-long defense mechanism -- oftentimes, running on auto-pilot.

In marked contrast, Satanists don't have this problem. Our egos are so self-based that they do not bear the fragility of those who garner ego-fulfillment from external influence and outside approval.

Even with that, the Satanist is indeed capable of admiring someone else for one or more personal qualities, and still remain with ego intact. Unlike the blind adoration and unproductive worship others invest in specific individuals, the Satanist takes critical admiration of quality (not personality) and selfishly betters himself or herself to achieve something of autonomous worth and which brings direct and deserved pleasure to the self. Such can be the difference between consumers and producers.

But, believe it or not, externalizing the Satanic ego can be healthy in one arena: through the contrived and mindful state of the ritual chamber. Beyond and in addition to the base foundation upon which we resonate, Satan represents each Satanist on an individual level, and in terms of Greater Magic, we call upon that force in ourselves through our alignment with the image -- the archetype -- of Satan via formalized psychodrama. Though this may seem contradictory to the uninitiated, it isn't since Satan isn't some impersonal and externally-created substitute, factory-made to redirect our egos. It *is*, however, a concept largely unfathomable to a society insistently content with self-projection instead of self-exploration.

In matters of manipulation, the Satanic Will is ever mindful of the big picture, or as Dr. LaVey once summarized, we "act, but don't participate." The distinction is important, and is often the reason why we view the herd with such scorn or amusement regarding their mischanneled egos. Many of the aforementioned outlets for herd ego-fulfillment can also be exploited by the Satanist on an objective level, all the while keeping the balance of reward in his or her favor.

But if you're a Satanist, you probably knew all that.

PRODUCER OR CONSUMER?
WHICH ONE ARE YOU?

Satanism is a religion for doers. It is a philosophy that upholds not only the standard of the strong, but of doing something with that strength and not just sitting around talking about it. Certainly, intellectual deconstruction has its place and purpose but, when all is said, it's what you do that matters. Anything else is inertia.

With the rise of the Internet, we have witnessed all too much talk (sometimes, in voluminous detail) from those gleefully claiming the title of Satanist, but falling dramatically shy of showing the goods. Nowhere is this more evident than online.

Even when you remove the obvious coattail riders and Satanic "reformers" from the mix, there are still plenty of faux Satanists -- yea, even many who carry the Crimson Card -- who do a whole lot of talk without any of the walk. Some feel that what amounts to hiding behind a keyboard and a computer screen is sufficient enough to take the Devil's Name, and then try to convince others of their purported sincerity, but never give Him adequate representation.

In simplest terms, they are consumers. Not merely the type who buy manufactured goods that the media tells them to, but those who harbor an actual, pervasive mentality that is all take and no give. They consume in the truest sense of the word and then tack Satanism onto it for effect in spite of contradicting ethics.

So, where do these self-appointed fans of the Devil shop for their wash-and-wear identity? More often than not, their quest brings them to our doorstep.

Oftentimes, it starts with the merchandise and is precipitated by some interest in darkly-inspired popular music. From there, they glut themselves with an entire showroom of Satanic media or just anything with a Baphomet on or in it: Quintessentials CDs, issues of *The Black Flame* and *Not Like Most*, the DVD release of *Satanis*, you name it. But when perusal of this material is exhausted, the fix remains unsatisfied and they often move on to more direct contact.

With an ISP account and a desire to take the easy way out, many of these fledgling types avoid reading *The Satanic Bible* (or simply do not read it critically, or need "help" with it) and instead run to areas of the Web that they assume will offer them the fast-food equivalent.

Message boards, particularly ones that count among their ranks some actual Satanists, provide this consumer with additional identity and ego-boosting. On this assumedly more level terrain, they can adopt (read: copy) ideas, concepts, terminology, and "pointers" from their betters, all the while contributing nothing in return, save for some transparently slavish praise, knee-jerk agreement, or the standard, unimaginative non-gem: "Uh, yeah, me too."

Those slightly above the monosyllabic responses often graduate to a level of "preaching to the choir" that defies logic. If they aren't putting forth established Satanic quotations as their own, then it's some absurd "convincing" routine that a blatantly Satanic concept is... well... Satanic. Unlike the Boy Scouts, we don't hand out Merit Badges, so save your breath and your posturing.

One of the main motivators behind some of this is often a juvenile reaction toward one of the God religions -- namely, Christianity. Not having any concrete form of power or notable ability in their own lives, they place an embarrassing degree of stock in being "the adversary." And, filtered through their lack of understanding the human animal and the way the world operates, this adversarial role manifests in some truly counterproductive and pointless forms. Somehow skipping the very Satanic practice of avoiding irritants you need not subject yourself to (did they even read The Eleven Satanic Rules of the Earth?), they dive headlong into "blasphemy" and ignorantly position an imaginary deity and his decreasingly effectual followers as "the big enemy" -- through such, gaining an illusory sense of purpose and personal power. In the end, they are merely inverse Christians, not Satanists.

Although many become disenchanted by the extensive dismissal given to them by actual Satanists and then project their consumer need onto the next available host (and the Internet has its share of pseudo-Satanic "groups" that serve a marvelous purpose in taking our refuse away from us), some are too braindead to grasp the obvious. They simply continue to delude themselves into thinking that they are part of something with which, according to the very overt and specific philosophy contained in our major tome, they are completely incompatible. At this point, they unknowingly resign themselves to being the laughingstock of whatever corner of Satanically-inspired cyberspace they inhabit.

Since they have no real purpose in Satanism on a compatibility level and, at the same time, probably won't leave the picture (at least, not entirely) due to their limited mental processing or their need for vicariously attaining identity through us, they should only feed at a cost, one that provides the real benefit to someone else besides them: the producer.

Unlike consumers, producers in Satanism are the real deal, be it through art, music, literature, business, or some gratifying endeavor of worth. We are the innovators, creators, and doers, and such is a product of our actual abilities and insights -- certainly not some spooky Halloween costume we don to impress the other partygoers.

We also recognize something that some may not: that the laws of nature create an immovable hierarchy, one that stratifies individuals according to intelligence and performance, and wearing a pentagram necklace or committing Electric Hellfire Club lyrics to memory won't change that reality. Dress yourselves up any way you like, but that's how it is.

As such, the producers know this reality from a mindfully removed position. We will gladly take your money, sell you the product, and pocket the revenue. You can cop your Satanic high in the privacy of your own home (and away from us), self-deceivingly revel in your imagined alignment, and make other people think you're somehow elect or misunderstood. Perhaps, you'll even find friends more gullible than you are to provide your malnourished ego with "oohs" and "ahhs" while Mom and Dad take up the remaining slack by providing the disapproval you so desperately but unadmittingly desire.

Sadly for you, what you simply cannot purchase along with those ritual items, music recordings, and books is an acknowledgment from us. We won't be your friend, your teacher, your wink-and-nod, or your security blanket. You are left with merchandise bearing ideas and implying qualities you may never be able to come near, match, or exceed, regardless of "effort." You may even one day come to this realization, discover your misgivings, and move on to other vistas. The exit door is always open.

And for those true Satanists both online and of the media-purchasing variety, we'll continue as we always have, indulging in mutually beneficial discussion, productively networking, and inspiring each other to produce, create, and bring into this world our own visions made flesh, the Is To Be that we know individually, while others serve their role as spectators.

POP GOES THE PRETENSE

Popular culture, as it is defined at any one point in time, is often held in contempt by the Satanist. And, on some very significant levels, it should be. Often enough, it carries with it a set of rigid behaviors, dress codes, and mentalities that are, at best, mindlessly collective, emotionally disposable, and painfully pervasive -- in short, unrelatable.

One manifestation of this so-called culture is what is commonly associated with pop music. And though greater divisions have arisen in the last few decades between whether or not someone listens to the musical form, there is also an additional yet often unseen element to the equation that bears illustration.

Hand in hand with the unquestioning fandom and blind adoration with pop music comes the equally mindless and impulsive condemnation from the dissenting side. It is my contention that both sides of this coin are suspect, and that the Third Side is so patently ignored.

What so many MTV automatons and faux freethinkers alike miss is that their behaviors are way too similar. In the face of their compulsive self-delusion, rarely do they see that their position is, more often than not, contrived and orchestrated by those around them.

It's one thing to say that a certain musical act does not appeal to you. But how many people (yes, even you anti-pop folks out there) actually bother to pay attention to how these preferences came about? Many times, these opposing factions feel the way they do because the body of authority which they accept has taken hold of their opinion-forming and dictated all too effortlessly not only what they should like but, perhaps more to the point, what they should *not* like. Since the tacit slavery of the pop music idolaters is so obvious as to be laughable, let's point that acumen at the other folks for a few pages.

Though often covered up with a thin veneer of anti-cool (which is merely just a modified form of "cool"), the militantly anti-pop people don't get routed out so quickly for their sizably slavish conduct. Typically, this is because they are firmly planted -- with little to no deviation -- in some music subculture whose main mode is to play the contrarian to pop music, often at all costs. The rules of their clique state that liking some other form is forbidden. Slave mentality, through and through. Let's call it what it is, shall we?

Unfortunately, some of these folks claim an association to Satanism. However, if they truly approached the Satanic philosophy critically, they would see the error of their ways. Or the error of adopting someone else's ways. Take your pick.

Certainly, Satan represents an archetype of rebellion. More exactly, he represents a position of mindful rebellion. The qualifier is crucial here. Rebelling against something for rebellion's sake is duly un-Satanic because it can allow the criteria for rebellion to be imposed upon you by someone else, be it the music industry, your favorite bands, your so-called friends, or whatever passes for popular or even slightly-unpopular culture.

Far too often, I've seen the opinions of others so thoroughly entrenched in social assimilation, whether they sport the latest fashions or a pentagram around their necks. For the latter, it would simply kill them to be in the same room with a CD playing of an artist upon whom their crowd has cast its disapproval. You can actually see the anger and indignation in their eyes, and over what? A cutesy girl pop artist? And often, it's not because of their own personal music tastes (if they can even claim sole ownership to that "taste," which I strongly doubt), but because they care far too much about what other people think of them. Either way, the impulse to care about public opinion in that manner and then act upon it is herdthink, ladies and gentlemen. No two ways around it.

And, ultimately, the question must surface: Why does it all matter so much? This brings us to another point.

The wannabe Satanist has, among other flaws, this translucence prefacing his or her invented Satanic probability. Put plainly, they are bad actors. They are the types who try so darn hard to avoid anything produced by the mainstream and popular culture that their obsessive behavior becomes just another form of counterproductive conformity. They are merely joining another mentality club and then confusing that with

Satanism and the Church of Satan.

Quite frankly, the Satanist can indeed enjoy a few products of the popular culture. The prime difference between a pop music-loving Satanist and your average pop-worshiper is that the Satanist is immune to the collective mindset and the consumer values often tacked onto pop music by the corporations and the media. It is the truly insecure that avoid pop music solely based upon this, and it should be obvious that such avoidance might be because, deep down, many of these anti-pop folks are as vulnerable to indoctrination but just don't want to admit it and don't trust themselves enough to be able to avoid it. To save face, this frail lot subscribe to another group, either music subcultural or even Satanism, to appear above it all.

Of course, there is also the possibility that some (and I stress the word, "some") anti-pop people are just really unhappy people. Even if you remove the pop listeners who are complete drones and are left with listeners who simply like the music, there will always be the sad sacks who feel compelled to denounce it. Again, why should they care? Allow me to clarify the potential excuses.

Another reason why some of the wannabes gravitate to Satanism is because there is an assumed chic to appearing against-the-grain. Although they'd be hard-pressed to admit it, what often lurks beneath is someone entertaining delusions of adequacy, thinly veiling inferior traits by relying on *ad hominem* attacks and memorized quotes from individuals to which they'll never measure up. In desperation, these types will rail against popular targets to feign discernment. Call it Little Man Syndrome. Or call it quack psychology -- as if somehow the music you listen to automatically assigns you to a predetermined social position of any importance. Not only do their insecurities make them vile, they make them petty and mischanneled therapy candidates!

Though alluded to before, there is also the identification factor. Yes, many pop followers have built their identities upon their favorite music celebrities, but so too have many of the anti-pop contingency. It is these unyielding, pre-processed roles which both types don that are convenient excuses for not thinking outside the box. These limitations foster not only stagnant thinking but also reinforce a strict adherence to dualism.

Regarding the entire bunch, I see little difference in the impetus behind their pointless "us vs. them" fixation as I do in the flaccid constructs of good and evil, left and right, black and white. Where is the

Third Side for these lost souls? Willingly renounced, apparently. They are tragically agreeing to a strain of Christianized thinking and probably don't even know it.

Such shortsightedness and all-out obedience to external directives are not the mark of the Satanist. Satanism is about enjoying life, indulging in the pleasures around us unrepentantly, all the while keeping a mindful eye to avoiding oppressive mentalities, to name a few. It's a cakewalk for the Alien Elite. Why isn't it for the rest of you?

ABSOLUTES CAN CORRUPT ABSOLUTELY

Death and taxes aside, there are very few absolutes in the world. In fact, that last statement might just be one of those few. Some of us learn this following our childhood, when the blinders are ripped away and previously assumed absolutes prove themselves to be mere inventions of man to keep the gears of civilization moving. From a social engineering standpoint, some are rather useful and serve to keep otherwise unstable and weak-minded people in check.

Other so-called absolutes, however, are largely useless and only work to keep many of the not-so-unstable people needlessly in lockstep with mindless conformity and away from certain types of confrontation -- in effect, reinforcing a childlike state, with the Powers That Be serving in the capacity of stern father. Life may be easier this way, but to the Satanist, it is little more than a position for slaves.

Much of the confusion has a profoundly causal link to others -- past or present -- who hastily force-apply a label to something that may not require it, or to malign a concept or condition for the sole purpose of convincing others that one has the positive solution to that condition, all to gain a certain status. Same game that many of the God religions play: in order to seem "good," they invent an "evil" in order to provide contrast to and, thus, bolster the semblance of this "good." Those who stray from this artificial duality (and especially succeed in persuading others to do likewise) are said to be a "corrupting" influence.

In Satanism, we champion actuality and bedrock knowledge in a world content with its delusions and superstitions. Deviation from this position -- such being over-reliance upon belief -- is, to us, corruption. The difference between the two is important: the God religions mostly claim their core beliefs as facts; whereas we demand facts when presented with beliefs. Ultimately, the burden of proof is in their corner and, as we've all witnessed, their jury's still out on that one.

So, let's explore some expressions of absolutism that so many take for granted, or simply are accepted at face value...

"I can get along with everybody."

The true mark of a cad. For an alarmingly large number in any given populace, lack of appropriate discrimination has gotten so far out of hand that the social climate often defaults to an assertion of everyone being "okay," regardless of the reality of the situation: that some people (many people, in the Satanist's viewpoint) are downright detestable and should be held accountable for such. Little wonder why it's the "people person" that Satanists find difficult to take seriously or truly admire, because if they can't be selective with those they include in their inner circle, then they might be indecisive and generally wishy-washy about much more important matters in their lives.

"I'll try anything."

More blatant spewage of verbal tripe. More often than not, this little non-gem is used to impress the other sheep, to make the quoter appear adventurous or daring, slathering on a thin veneer of perceived importance, or even relevance. Unfortunately, the mentally challenged majority of people buy into this bankrupt braggadocio, probably because they can then use it at their next bar hop or keg party to increase their own social position (which is actually important to them outside of pragmatic reasons -- pity them).

Taken to a realistic level, not one of these types would do "anything." In fact, it is my contention that this "rebel" spirit of theirs is largely consigned to quasi-acceptable social activities such as breast-flashing, "body" shots, and drunken Karaoke. I can think of at least one thing they probably wouldn't try: it's called thinking for themselves!

Also, as self-preservationists, we Satanists know that "anything" shouldn't necessarily be tried. Pragmatism, empiricism, and mindfulness are the tools we generally use to gauge our situations -- often with far more advantageous and ultimately joyful results than of those who merely "jump right in."

"You can do (or be) anything you want in life."

Wrong, no, untrue, balderdash, and poppycock! This is merely one more attempt at propagating the myth of "equality" for all, something that never seems to wear thin with the uninspired and generally unfit of our great planet. It should be a no-brainer that each individual is limited to potential and achievement levels commensurate with their intelligence and performance. More to the point, not everyone is an evolved being (let alone a Satanist, for that matter), but somehow this doesn't stop many folks from making spectacles of themselves by trying to exceed beyond their immovable limitations. No wonder so many of them grow up bitter and unsatisfied, not to mention oblivious to the Balance Factor (see: *The Satanic Bible*, p. 127).

"I have good morals."

Define "good" and define "morals." Both are irrefutably subjective terms for which the mindless masses have so illogically and projectingly deemed absolutes. Typically, this type of thinking is what locks people into such a state of relative solipsism that nothing is real outside the confines of their cultural norms, and what in excessive cases leads to racism, sexism, homophobia, and an adherence to a patchwork of other deleterious, two-dimensional social constructs.

The term "moral" is also a prime tool used by many Christians and the like to integrate their specific value system into secular society. This is well-exemplified by the use of terms normally open to inclusion, but are instead used to exclude. These include "God" (as if there are no others), "bible" (from the Latin root for "book"... again, as if there are no other books above theirs), "values" (which often fall into the strict parameters of Christianity, but are assumed to be the law of the land), and, of course, "morals." Since Satan is the archetype of accuser or questioner of all things, it follows that questioning even the most assumed values and established terms in our society is a healthy, productive, and Satanic activity.

"You are corrupting the youth of America."

This simply must follow the preceding example in terms of process. The key word in this quote is "corrupting." The subtext of this example, or what is more than implied to those aware, is that there must be some supposed default condition for the youth (3-year-olds? Teens? Does it matter to some?) and that any deviation, as mentioned before, from this arbitrary assignation is grounds for being labeled "corruption." Most people don't view it that way because to do so would be to admit to some unchecked indoctrination (or intentional yet covert social engineering), but that's exactly what is being conveyed in the example. The gist is thus: don't color outside the lines, don't discuss social conditions in a way to which the herd can't relate, and by all means, don't eat that pesky Fruit of Knowledge.

"I should be treated like a king (or queen) by women (or men)."

If by dint of being a human being, you claim that you merit exceptional consideration from others, then allow me to inform you that you are as deluded as they come. More exactly, the implication that mere biology grants one the universal right of unconditional respect is patently unfounded, insulting to legitimate relationships, and suggestive of someone lacking critical thought.

Gladfully, the bulk of the world doesn't work this way. The Satanist knows all too well that the most meaningful relationships are the ones in which all involved parties have earned appreciation and respect through actual achievement and accurate representation, and not as a result of unrealistic personal assessment.

Some people deserve to be treated well. Others allow themselves to be treated like chattel. Tis the order of nature: each of you deserves that to which you consign yourself. A brutal call, and the only realistic one to make.

"Can't we all just get along?"

No. Absolutely not.

"That's just common sense."

Before one can even deal with this statement, the word "sense" must be properly defined. If by "sense," we mean that knowledge and reason, used productively, bring a person to fruitful conclusions, then I've got news for the world: common sense is far from being common.

Of course, what many mean when they use the term is that some specific social construct (ex.: "Having an abortion is wrong!") should be considered innate or natural to people. This, again, is when assumptions are deceitfully conveyed as inherent, or absolute. It also implies that everyone should be on the same page -- or is capable of being on the same page, as the "equality" lie dictates.

"I'm an open-minded person."

Yet another expression that means different things to different people. But, for many, it simply means unquestioning acceptance of things regarding other people and events. Though the intention can often be noble, what "open-mindedness" often results in is a whole lot of fence-sitting and ambivalence, and certainly not tempered with critical thinking, something that would make open-mindedness an actually useful implement. Of course, it also helps if the brain you are thinking with is of reasonable quality.

Conversely, the term, "close-minded" is often abused and used by people towards those with whom they simply don't agree. For them, saying "you're close-minded" instead of "I don't agree with you" seems to carry more authority with the accuser, cheap and flimsy as it really is. Talk about lack of perspective!

"I have rights, damnit!"

No, you have legislated privileges enforced and maintained by a government and a military (much like man-made "laws" being, in actuality, legislated rules). When these artificial systems are not in place, you have only the rights you maintain by wit or by force -- or, perhaps more effectively, by both. Therefore, a right is an extremely amorphous concept at best within the cultural milieu. It's when the bleating of the human sheep echoes the transparent sentiment that we all have "rights" as people -- again, simply by being alive -- shows their inability to survive without some other larger entity looking over them, be it government or an assumed "God." These "rights" aren't necessarily useless or "bad," but let's know them for what they are.

"My love for you is unconditional."

Ultimately, I'm more than convinced that unconditional love is a patent fiction and, as a Satanist, I don't see anything realistic or productive in assuming that such a thing does or even should actually exist, "real" or otherwise. Of course, love (in all of its multitudinous forms) is highly conditional. Though the conditions may and certainly do vary from person to person, our primary needs and wants expect reciprocity -- particularly from those we hold as significant others and those in which we invest mindful love. For example, my conditions for a romantic partner consist of camaraderie, some meaningful common ground, fidelity, respect for who I am, and a host of others. Remove those from the equation and it is simply not romantic love for me nor anything I wish to deem as such. Considering we all work on a relative plane (though with some differing criteria), love will always be conditional. Otherwise, it becomes a formless, meaningless, "love"-everyone gesture devoid of clear-sightedness and self-respect. It's no accident that Satanism embraces loving and hating those who deserve such. Those are staunch and unflinching judgments utilized by the Higher Man (and Woman). As it should be. The further one gets from the herd fantasy of unconditional love, the closer one gets to not only understanding his or her personal desires but, as a result, often attracts those who resonate with and reflect back many of those same standards, all the while personally understanding that dynamic and appreciating it all far more than those who throw their affections and attachments around as if so much confetti.

In far too many cases, the excess of this unrealistic belief in unconditional love has welcomed the herd to such consequences as tolerated domestic violence (and tolerated child abuse... on any relative end), ongoing emotional dissatisfaction, resentfully-endured infidelity, and the forcing upon others of counterproductively selfish demands (and don't think for a second that Christianity and at least one other God religion didn't have a marked hand in encouraging this so-called "love" in American culture -- as well as in others -- yet conveniently don't get sufficiently brought to task for the negative impact of these extreme but often inevitable outcomes). Count me out.

Probably the most revealing aspect of all of these supposed absolutes, and in stark contrast to the mindsets that the adherents to them all seem to have in common, is that much of the remainder of the animal kingdom really doesn't share this form of self-deception. Neither does the Satanist... and rightfully so, since we acknowledge and uphold our animal nature while most people try so desperately to shed theirs and deny it. To parallel, non-human animals consistently live in reality: they recognize pain and pleasure and know the difference, danger is always real and not merely a concept, and relations with others (either of the interspecies type or not) are based upon experience and not memorized social dictates. The world isn't black and white for either us or the non-human animals because the latter can't afford to entertain such nonsense and we as Satanists possess the ability to see through the so-called absolutes intellectually, know through our greater access to our instincts that said examples are a sham, and with both instinct and intellect in balance, we act or react productively.

So, while many of those on the outside continue to swim gleefully in their own limited thinking and obedience to impersonal cultural precepts, the Satanist will ever rise above the morass with both little effort and open eyes.

LOVE IS A MANY CONDITIONAL THING

For many centuries -- particularly those during which many people have existed in civilized cultures -- the myth of unconditional love has served as a salve for the otherwise unlovable, the inept, and the weak of mind. It is a human construct that trembles in fear when reality intrudes upon it, and crumbles when met with a truly rational mind. Like the God religions which propagate this myth, its only real purposes are to enforce, pacify, and distract.

The correlation between unconditional love and the God religions is all too apparent to those who do not truly subscribe to either. Christianity, being one of the more visible God religions in Western culture, makes the spurious claim that unconditional love is handed down by their central deity -- thus, providing an example to emulate. Putting aside the ludicrous assertion that a God literally exists to begin with, let's approach this from the perspective of the actual believer for a moment. According to Christians, the Bible is the definitive work of their religion and is directly given to them by their God. Knowing that, it takes a huge amount of "selective" reading to avoid the voluminous accounts of claimed condemnation, judgment, and acceptance/rejection from this assumed entity towards mankind, regardless of modern "revisionist" texts that offer more backpedaling and apologies than adherence to established scriptural context. Keeping with the mythology, God's love is highly conditional -- otherwise, plagues, damnation, world floods, death by fiery serpents, and rejection from thy heavenly area would not be part of the "divine plan."

By an odd contrast, many supporters of UL use the above emulation paradigm as a "negative" example of why we should subscribe to unconditional love all the more. Largely, it comes from knee-jerk atheists and agnostics who are dissatisfied with the structure of these religions but unknowingly (or self-denyingly) subscribe to their shared fundamentals. The rigidly dualistic thinking here is either the choice to resign one's Will to an externalized god, or to resign oneself to the Will of a relationship partner. The Third Side of this argument is completely avoided: outside of submission and denial is also the option of removing the relationship altogether, if even entered at all. Since many people cling to the concept of love so desperately, the thought of jettisoning counterproductive and even harmful relationships strikes such terror into their lonely hearts that the reaction is to lock themselves into the submission-or-denial trap even more tightly. Unlike the contradictory "God" model illustrated in the previous paragraph, this ignorance of the Third Side is clearly inherent to the God religions and their theology. Other God-religious reinforcements for UL include the "do unto others" and "love thy brother" values, the purported "salvation" achieved through the vain attempt at practicing UL, and the myth of equality that is the crux of the God religions.

Make no mistake. The myth of equality is at the fore of UL. Once someone tries to love another without met expectations and placing all love on an equal playing field, it is reduced to a mediocre and worthless concept, devoid of any real definition and leaving the practitioner open to the dangerous notion that anything anyone does in a relationship is acceptable, whether it takes the form of sexual violation, betrayal, physical abuse, emotional cruelty, infidelity, unreasonable demands, or a wealth of crucial incompatibilities. And it is all reinforced by a belief-centered adherence to UL, notably comparable to that of certain religious belief forms.

Where matters get even more convoluted for adherents to UL is the entirely misguided idea that UL fosters self-acceptance. Even aside from the fact that needing something external to validate a person is both weak and worthy of contempt, following the tenets of UL do not lead one to self-acceptance, they lead to self-denial.

Often enough, this self-denial is made manifest in the area of compromise. As it stands, compromise is not an absolutely counterproductive practice, and moments of reasonable forms may be necessary. But, when compromise solely benefits the other person and not also the practitioner, either in a personal or practical sense, is when the line is crossed into self-denial.

Unfortunately, there have been voices in the social science community that have lent absurd credence to this idea of UL. Psychologists Alfred Adler (1870-1937) and Abraham Maslow (1908-1970) considered unconditional love to be a part of basic human needs, essential to a person's well-being. And while love itself may be necessary, UL categorically denies many individual needs while the participant submits to needs in others that conflict with their own at the same time. The theory presented by these gentlemen is a fantasy whose roots are grounded in the artificial constructs of civilized society -- a society that often runs counter to productive animal nature -- and do not hold up once belief is eliminated.

Even those in the worlds of criminology and law enforcement push the UL card when dealing with the social aspects of criminals. Apologist arguments surface to the tune of crime being the main product of not receiving UL, which whitewashes away personal responsibility to an embarrassing degree. Much like getting prisoners to take up a belief in Jesus, the (re)introduction of the UL concept for released prisoners and their probationary ilk is used as an intended deterrent to recidivism. Perhaps a useful social maintenance tool to deal with the weak-minded, but, again, not exactly rooted in reality. Merely another example of belief indoctrination.

Again, presuppositions arise in these frail arguments for UL: that a person's worth is based on others (or the acceptance from others), that belief is fact, and that we cannot survive without these constructs that "we" humans have made.

Which brings in the control factor. Again, as another form of irrational belief, love by these types is not only assumed to be unconditional (read: absolute), but also out of their control. "We don't choose who we love or how much," says the slave. Hogwash!

Of course, we can control who we love and to what extent. It's just that some choose not to, and then either accept whatever is put on their plate or needlessly complain about it without taking steps to actually remedy the situation. The first is resignation. The second is stupidity. And both are purely voluntary.

Accepting this resignation and stupidly -- often products of lazy thinking, if any -- often leads to another undesirable element: dependency. Sadly, many of the herd define themselves by their relationships, and not always by the quality of them but just by having one. Inside all of that, individual will is lost, and the participants submit not only to the Will of each other, but both to an assumedly greater Will: that of the concept of "love" itself. In this arena, UL becomes a god -- one that demands absolute obedience, no questions, and a sizable denial of self from others. Sensing a pattern here?

And although this pattern can be more directly linked to a religious model, it also has secular roots in modern culture. Social expectations on what each prescribed "form" of love is supposed to be are, by the many, falsely considered the nature of the beast, and are often unknowingly derived from unexamined behavioral modeling from others around them, be they real or fiction. In this specific aspect of love, the conditions are pre-determined by social templates and voluntarily used by those who prefer tradition to effective communication. Since these conditions are not viewed by the many as such, the illusion of UL can still be entertained by those in desperate need of it.

Even individuals who claim emancipation from the UL game might still hold to the idea of polyamory being proof of unconditional love. Whether polyamory is for sexual or emotional reasons, UL is still an unrealistic alternative, even more so since more than two people are involved. Discrimination must be practiced to an even greater extent to keep such a relationship productive, honest, and gratifying, and the complex interconnections of wants and needs beyond traditional monogamy require further conditions. Merely that there may be less traditional conditions in a polyamorous arrangement, let alone any relationship, does not mean that there are none.

Fortunately, most people simply do not subscribe to totally unconditional love -- but many of them sure do like self-ascribing the term. Stating their relationships as being unconditional allows them some semblance of achievement (often, in the place of real life achievement) or that it was "meant to be" -- sometimes by imaginary concepts like fate, karma, Cupid, or a god. It affords them that all-too-familiar Good-guy Badge that they can polish up for cocktail parties and PTA meetings, while their relationships contain plenty of very real conditions, either productive or nay. Consider it an intricate web of deceit that can even entangle its spinners.

Small wonder why UL is incompatible with Satanism. We know that healthy emotional investment is both conditional and tentative, and reliant upon reciprocity. After examining each situation carefully, we give our sentiments to those who have proven themselves to be worthy of them. They, in turn, should respond in kind. All else is error.

We are also not reliant upon outside approval to enjoy our lives.

We are fiercely independent and reserve our giving of respect for those who both recognize that independence in us and possess it themselves. Relationships for us are complementary and selective, rather than mere socially expected conventions and exercises in unadmitted masochism. We do not need a God-substitute wrapped up in pretty secular packaging to serve as the rules of relationship making and maintenance. As an extension of Satanism itself, our relationships are composed of mindful alignment, a resonance that represents the balance of nature rather than being at odds with it. And understanding nature and its deeper implications is at the heart of the religion we call Satanism.

DATING OUTSIDE YOUR RACE

The dating ritual, whether it is dictated by the dominant culture or dependent upon your own discrimination, is a dicey thing at best. Elements both seen and unseen play a role, but knowing the difference between a person of worth and someone who merely looks really great is the steadfast aim of any Satanist keeping an open eye to vital prospects.

Hanging above like some sickly vulture is the herd criteria for romantic compatibility: "I'm attracted to her, I like having sex with her, we get along, and I like our conversations -- therefore, this is love." And it is this grade-school equation whose sum is a little more than suspect to the Satanist. So much so that we know when to avoid the lackluster and shallow made-for-movie version of love that the herd so tragically wrap themselves in. And we also know with absolute certainty that they are not the directors of these insipid celluloid disasters but the audience members witlessly acting out the roles handed to them. As is often the case, even a basic level of self-discipline escapes them.

One occurrence that elicits the fervent headshake and eye-roll from me is the suspension of individuality among many herd relationship participants -- encapsulated in the disturbingly widespread phrase, "when two become one." Akin to some bad 1950s Sci-Fi movie plot, they unquestioningly absorb each other's personalities, likes, dispositions, etc. -- and probably for a few reasons, none of which admirable. Women who swore up and down previous to the relationship that they found total and unswerving disgust in a certain viewpoint all of a sudden "really love it now" -- and definitely not as a result of some well-pondered education. Men who extensively and very vocally tore apart ladies (if heterosexual) with a certain extreme body archetype -- skinny or voluptuous -- now praise it endlessly and claim it superior, all because "she" has it, but after the (even amicable) end of the romance, resume tearing it to shreds until the next gal with the same body type catches his fancy, and the ludicrous cycle begins again. Dogs chase their own tails, too, but something tells me that our canine friends are actually doing that for fun.

Also of note are the laughable power struggles. If these people actually used their brains, the energy and motivation behind these struggles could be channeled into bettering their lives in matters of career and intellectual advancement rather than a lifelong pissing contest intermittently paused for brief sexual activity. Without fail, few situations reveal just how weak and subservient some people are than in a love affair bonded by attraction disparity, in which many of the struggles are established. In laymen's terms, one person is conventionally (or perceivedly) more attractive or of higher quality in some notable area than the other. He (or, often enough, she) who has the gold makes the rules, and that applies specifically to these types. So, I sit back and enjoy the show of manipulation, personality molding, testing of boundaries, and an assortment of general trickery that is more than telling -- on *both* sides.

Even before all of this nonsense, it's painfully apparent that a lot of people get into romantic relationships for some incredibly stupid reasons. Staggeringly stupid reasons. As intelligent and observant outsiders, many Satanists can say that they possess a mental log of the herd's moronically reductive approaches for sheer entertainment, and new ones are no doubt added all the time. Though the re-runs are still hilarious: insecurity, identity, loneliness, possessiveness, lack of personal power, ulterior motives, and the list goes on.

Out of all of these, the one which either garners mindless sympathy or generates a great deal of insecure drama is loneliness. Looking down upon the herd, I truly wonder what they're complaining about. For the most part, the bulk of humanity is not truly lonely at all, either companionwise or in the romantic/sexual department. When the pleas for attention and other grandstanding are cleared away, much of their gripes are either unadmitted (or mischanneled) sexual tension or some insecure drive to be "needed" (whatever that means to any one person and, evidently, at any cost). Or, it's simply that they are really screwed up people who have yet to legitimately strive toward solving their own issues. True loneliness couldn't possibly be the reality of the many because they ARE the many -- their shared wellspring of popular culture in all of its forms, comparatively unquestioned but commonly cherished ethics and values, and overall indiscrimination in regards to chosen company guarantees their pairing and relative compatibility. Put simply, they are far more like each other than is often admitted.

The standard response to my claims is often, "Well, I'm lonely but I'm not alone." What does such indiscrimination feel like? The fact that warm bodies in people's lives are ultimately good enough and then defended as "meaningful" is nauseating. Conversely, the ideal that quality actually matters more than quantity -- and the brains to know the difference -- is a true blasphemy in a disposable, consumer-minded culture, which explains (but doesn't really validate) quite a bit of the confusion.

More often than not, when I hear cries of, "Oh, I'm so lonely," I'm torn between amusement and disgust. Because it often comes from such an excessively insincere place.

What comes from the flipside of all of this is equally telling: that of the social stigma attached to those even assumed to be lonely. In many cultures, a romantic relationship (for example) becomes some sort of Merit Badge for far too many folks, an accomplishment akin to a successful career or any other comparative achievement. Again, the consumer-cultural influence emerges, which manifests as solipsism personally misread as universal factuality. That is, those who have one of these relationships can perceive themselves as somehow "better" than those who do not (which immediately makes me theorize where the lack of real accomplishments in their lives resides, and if this isn't just a convenient diversion from such being revealed, to others or even themselves). What gets lost in the translation is the evidence mentioned above, that dominant cultural commonality pairs the majority so easily and that anyone not of that commonality is read as not being able to "acquire" the same. And I use the term, "acquire" intentionally because it truly captures the attitude of these types. How any culture can support the absurd notion that something involving the mutual establishment of two people being instead the accomplishment of one person is mindboggling. Then again, so is the adoption of hyphenated last names. Please stop that, by the way.

All of this, among other realities, assigns the Satanist to a unique and advantageous position. We are inarguably a race apart, a tribe of critical rebels and explorers of what is truly occult (read: hidden). As such, we are masters at ferreting out the unspoken agendas of disingenuous applicants. Most likely because many of us have repeatedly witnessed the same manipulation rampant amongst the converts of the

God religions, plying the less erudite with warm fuzzy feelings, the semblance of "belonging" and a purportedly eternal love affair with Jesus. Same shtick, same lack of awareness, same enslavement. Hallmark merely changes the names on the cards.

Of course, this unique and advantageous position of ours is found rather attractive by numerous lessers who are too draining to even consider including in our lives past the act of coitus -- if even before that. These are the individuals who smell power and confidence on someone and, in an attempt to acquire the same, latch on and commence feeding like the psychic vampires they are. And they are out there -- in droves. Whether they are pseudo-Satanists (even the CoS card-carrying variety) chasing after some vicarious thrill derived from intimate dealings with a titled CoS member, or your garden variety adherents to some dark subculture looking to up their spook cred, they are compelled by their need to be more than they are by taking those sought-after qualities from you. Don't permit them to.

If you are among the number of single Satanists open to the possibility of a romantic relationship, you have a lot more to think about than those who seem to not do a whole lot of thinking in this same department. By our very nature, we are free of such herd restraints as needing someone to make us feel "whole" or "valid." We avoid pairing up because of social or other outside expectations -- practices that are still very much a reality for others out there. It is also true that the Satanist has no need for strict traditional definitions of relationship, marriage, or family -- unless it's productive and mutually ego-gratifying to include them. But, what we don't desire is entering into a life situation -- especially one this crucial -- without some razor-sharp astuteness and evaluation before the fact.

Against all of the flighty herd propaganda to the contrary, it is the practical choice of the dating-minded Satanist to cut away the inferior possibilities and wait for that person who resonates with the Black Flame that we hold dear. The embodiment of the Satanic or even anything reasonably close to it is truly uncommon, and to compromise too much is to poison the self so profoundly with all of the irresponsibilities and superficial qualities of these others that such hastily considered ventures simply aren't worth it. We want meaningful unions which will both add to our lives and, if applicable, result in the most appropriate selection for contributing to the bearing of our progeny -- a choice we make with far more consideration and seriousness than many non-Satanists, whose reckless breeding habits are both evident and appalling. In all aspects of life, we demand value for value given and not simply settling for whatever is dumped on our plates. Anything less than reciprocity is an insult to ourselves and our standards.

LET'S HEAR IT FOR SEXUAL OBJECTIFICATION

Any Satanist who steps outside his lair cannot help being stormed by the end-products of a near-neutered (or semi-spayed, if more to your liking) culture. It seems the modern proselytizers of militant anti-sex doctrine, whether from the carnally-frustrated Religious Right or the Salem Male Trials inquisitors of "feminist" extremism, have taken occasional root over the span of the post-Church of Satan years (i.e.: after 1966). Throughout these decades, we've unswervingly supported and even glorified woman's productive use of her natural manipulative instincts to improve her circumstances; and evidently, the formula often works as any glance at network and cable TV (to name just a couple) will show. No doubt, detractors of sexual objectification, voluntarily blind to who really holds the cards, would find our brand of female empowerment as an indirect form of male control over womankind, or just plain "sexist."

Nothing more than the complete opposite is true, but where you stand on whether or not sexual objectification is a productive and beneficial outcome depends a great deal on whether you are a Have or a Have-not.

In the overwhelmingly large number of cases, those shouting the loudest against the portrayal of women (or even men, though we don't see much protest of that, now do we?) as sex objects, particularly those offered by the media, are usually nature's less-endowed specimens. But, instead of being secure with themselves and finding another way to attain success in the world (such as through intellectual means) or improving what part of their physical lot they can (and this is not limited to weight loss and cosmetic surgery), a Holy War is waged upon the Sexy for merely being resourceful with their lusty attributes; a heinous crime in this slobberingly egalitarian day and age.

Isn't the consistency of pretentious victim-play just a bit too thick to swallow? Or is it that some sexual persecutors (and anti-sex objectifiers are one form) desire the position of social autocrat -- preaching to men what they are permitted to enjoy looking at, and dictating to women what they may and may not wear (let alone the reason for wearing it)? If the anti-exploiters would allow the smoke to clear from their view, they'd see the futility in their campaign: that what they propose is rabidly anti-nature, and it is impossible to muzzle or regulate the natural sexual behavior of either gender when it's so far out of grasp. The effort proves the anti-objectifiers to be insecure, stupid, and mindlessly power-tripping. Same trap as evangelical Christianity.

The hypocrisy of some of the most flagrantly vocal "free speech", "pro-woman" and "First Amendment" groups practically rallying for the banning and censorship of images of sexually-objectified people (or is it just women?) is not only playing the respective enemy's game, but a outright embarrassment. To these types, freedom for a woman to choose to abort a fetus within her own body is good, freedom to self-exploit that same body is bad. Some folks should make up their minds.

I say cheers to sexual objectification! It sure beats sexual repression. And people crave such voyeuristic stimulation, otherwise mainstream media, fashion, and the porn industry wouldn't be the billion-dollar businesses that they are. Sexual objectification sells... and sells well; a clear indicator that there is something to it, an appeal to a pervasive and important human desire. Many women have such a wonderfully diabolical gift of being able to prosper from their sexual appeal and, by that wielding, show themselves to be very powerful, strong and in-control beings. This makes more sense to label feminism than what passes for it currently. And, I'm certainly not the first one to say this.

My favorite fallacy concerning the effects of supposed "violent" imagery of women objectified is that this significantly influences men to go out and replicate. This is hardly the majority of men. To think this is to over-intellectualize away the simplicity of the situation. If you took the average man and put in front of him a picture of a greased, naked woman on all-fours with a dog collar around her neck, a man's hand holding the leash, and having a black glove shoved in her face to sniff, Joe Average would, more times than not, take one look and say something to the effect of "Hey, nice beave!" Objectification (or maybe just plain horny), yes. Future violent offender, stretching the point.

Let's Hear It For Sexual Objectification

Sexual objectification is woven deep into our very urges; particularly, the ones that are stimulated by seeing something or someone attractive. We are visual creatures, regardless of how the God religions and the politically-correct slaves try to discount or trivialize it. We (especially, but not limited to, men) have a natural inclination to be sexually aroused by visuals. The Powers-That-Can't would have us believe that this is "evil," if you haven't heard that buzzword before.

I'm sickened to death of hearing how I should be attracted to someone solely for their mind. What a load of apologist crap. What a Have-notism! And without the soothing, popularist rhetoric getting in the way of a point, like it always does, this mind-before-body ploy (also known as "but she has a really nice personality") is merely a means to sanction those less fortunate a reserved end of the coitus pool. An intellectually superior brain, though useful in nearly every other aspect of human life, isn't really a prerequisite for fornication or even a decent blowjob. So, go have some big, dumb sex.

This isn't to say, however, that body plus mind isn't a far more effective equation in the long run. As reason has it, it is. Women who have the physical plumage to attract often do better by having the brains to keep it going and profit for a prolonged period of time. Again, it's often enough the combination of the both ugly and stupid of the feminine ranks who resent the former, and they do so with the transparent pretext that most human bottom feeders display. Such is the struggle for survival.

To say sexual objectification is "wrong" is to say that the act of being attracted physically to another person is also "wrong." It is both hypocritical and projecting, not to mention silly. Whether money is made from it or not, the archetype of the sex object will stand proud as both a testimony to our productive animal nature and a taskmaster to correct the herd's collective denial of pure attraction.

Absolute Human Companions: A Practical Inquiry

"Development and Production of Artificial Human Companions -- The forbidden industry. An economic 'godsend' which will allow everyone 'power' over someone else. Polite, sophisticated, technologically feasible slavery. And the most profitable industry since TV and the computer."

- from "Pentagonal Revisionism: A Five-Point Program" by Anton Szandor LaVey

Like many of Dr. LaVey's ideas, the concept of Artificial Human Companions is often met by the masses with apprehension, confusion, and the occasional knee-jerk condemnation. To those of them who can muster the individual mental processing to get past the unconventionality of the idea, perhaps many would really enjoy the ownership of an AHC, and for myriad uses, each tailored to their particular desires. It could also elicit potential redefinition for such concepts as friendship, love, and consciousness, as is illustrated in the 2001 Spielberg film, *Artificial Intelligence: A.I.* When combined with the growing interest in personal technology as practical application, it certainly isn't only Satanists that are exploring the conceptual possibilities of greater interactivity with artifice in the 21st century.

One manifestation of AHCs on a primitive but promising level is that of the Real Doll (www.realdoll.com). And although their function is primarily sexual in design, their reasonably realistic sculpting, joint inclusion, and carnal accommodations are certainly a step into a Pygmalion realm, a Satanic realm which places man in the role of a god exercising both creation and dominion. Soon, these fledgling AHCs will purportedly possess programmable animatronic response and, with the inevitable advancement in computer technology, it seems feasible that they may one day be able to mimic behavioral response, follow commands, and perhaps even find themselves endowed with something along the lines of an inorganic consciousness (if the last is desired by the specific owner, at which point the "ownership" role may have to be reassessed).

Naturally, the alarmists and the religiously insecure will hobble to the fore with cries of "Well, what then stops us from making slaves of *real* people?" Although this type of "slippery slope" thinking is intellectually dismissible on the grounds that the separation of what's real and what's fantasy can be observed during one day at Disney World (or by being allowed visitation to a Total Environment created by a Satanist), others might begin wondering about the practical application of genetically created slaves.

If actually entertaining the notion of genetic slaves for either personal amusement or actuality, a major concern would be dealing with the potential hornet's nest this practice would provoke. Some matters of consideration that could or probably would emerge...

1) The issue of Free Will. Unless this could be short-circuited in a human genetic creation (and good luck on that one, since human consciousness has yet to be mapped or sizably understood to this day outside of it having something to do with reason), an organic slave could sooner or later discover the desire for autonomy as the *de facto* child that he or she would probably be. Once many of them discover discontent for slavery on their own, they may eventually bite the hand that feeds them, or far worse as the motion picture, *Blade Runner* aptly conveys with mere androids. With actual humans, picture a bloody revolution to rival and perhaps exceed any significant uprising in recorded history.

2) Automata are less troublesome in that they could lack many of the conventional inconveniences of an organic slave. Regarding the latter, extreme genetic modification would have to take place in order to maintain obedience and, conversely, discourage autonomy -- alterations such as focused (or absent) sexuality, sterilization, absolute immunization, removing the desire for external relationships, and a host of others. Also, unlike inorganic entities, organic slaves would require food, housing, and other monetary concerns.

3) Redefinition on the most basic level of human discourse, hierarchy, and value. Put plainly, society would have to be completely reorganized, restructured, and prepared somehow to accept such human recategorization, which could take decades, generations, or more to establish. As it stands, most people would have a huge problem with human slavery re-entering the picture at this point in time (if ever), and that would be a Herculean task to overcome in and of itself. You could say that it's none of their business, but they'll make it their business -- and it could get messy. By contrast, the public's acclimation to AHCs would involve a far easier, quicker, and more attractive marketing campaign by those with the power of social engineering.

Within the Satanic philosophy, conflict would also arise. Organic slaves could be made to be largely compliant but, in the final analysis, they are still human. Doing unto others as they do unto you couldn't be practiced in a master / slave relationship between humans because the human slave wouldn't be allowed reciprocity or even a relatively equal exchange. Stratification would be reduced to a fragile and potentially disastrous human construct, such as it became in the past, not to mention a system that counters the very human potential which we as Satanists champion.

Even if, on an intelligence level, the organic slave were on par with a child or a non-human animal, Satanism mindfully recognizes and respects both as being closer to their own nature -- something many human adults of the herd try to ignore in themselves. Keeping this in mind, the organic slave would have to be considered in a comparative light and would not be a suitable AHC substitute.

And since they are still of our species, disposal of them would still constitute murder (though, the Satanic exception could be made for the taking of a life as a last resort method of self-defense. But, even this act must take into account the laws of the State). A true AHC, being a machine, could be switched off, scrapped, reprogrammed, or physically modified when the owner is annoyed with it, or simply bored at the moment. It is not dehumanized because it is never human to begin with (outside of the "Intellectual Decompression" of role-playing). Though, if AHCs ever acquire what we'd consider a "consciousness," additional considerations will have to enter the picture in this particular instance.

All things considered, the development and manufacturing of AHCs, from a purely practical standpoint, solves the inherent problems that would come with organic substitutes. Dr. LaVey, in his putting forth of such groundbreaking ideas as AHCs and Total Environments, more than implies not only an understanding that keeping interactive artifice rationally apart from real life provides man with a healthy psychological release (much like ritual) but, also, that such keeps the lines drawn. Organic slaves could defeat the purpose, the very beneficial and productive division between the two -- and exponentially so with the masses and their often lax reasoning and disastrously associative conclusions.

Empirical evidence lending, the world is increasingly ready for the introduction of Artificial Human Companions, and technology is catching up with this eventual demand. The Internet has now become such an important and integral part of people's lives (for better or worse) around the world, particularly in matters of interactivity such as message boards and chat rooms, that the next logical step must be to increase the "realism" of human/ synthetic interaction that mere text-based conversation from faceless humans may not satisfy. The push for "bigger" and "better" by tech-savvy consumers (and this includes Internet users) will provide the demand for realistic people-substitutes sooner or later. Perhaps, even substitution to the point where the generally inept "real" people will have to keep up with and even attempt to surpass the potential wit, charm, and personality of their artificial betters, thus propelling our various cultures to the next step of social and personal progress.

Ever forward, indeed!

The Misanthrope's Survival Guide

One reality in the lives of many (if not all) Satanists, to some degree or another, is that of a mindful disdain for the masses. Much of what passes for "culture" is so spoonfed and impersonal, it would naturally disinterest individuals who highly value their autonomy and rational self-interest, and the outcome can be a generally misanthropic stance. And this is not necessarily limited to the specific overabundance of herd numbers but also that the intolerance meter can soar when factors such as attitudes, desires, ethics, behaviors, priorities, and the bulk of what rides shotgun to consumer culture is added to the mix.

Seeing as Satanists are Epicureans by nature, we seek to avoid or minimize interactions and experiences not found to be pleasurable, knowing full well that the majority of our interests are not shared with most. If properly thought out, a sizable amount of exposure can be lessened or completely eradicated, leaving the Satanist with more time to pursue either more solitary activities or those with the cherished few we intentionally select as social partners. The following are general guidelines to aid in that pursuit. (As supplement, I would also recommend "The Art of Invisibility" from *Satan Speaks!* by Anton Szandor LaVey.)

Groceries: The first order of business is self-preservation -- that is, sustenance. The secret to minimized exposure is to go at times when the places aren't busy. Take a look through your local phone book and seek out the 24-hour stores, planning to shop later at night. If you are nocturnal, this schedule would be to your advantage, particularly if you plan your shopping between the hours of 3 a.m. - 5 a.m., and generally only between Sunday and Thursday, which should clear out the drunks, the college kids, and, especially, the drunk college kids.

Also helpful whether or not you can shop late can be the use of what many modern grocery stores are providing, which is self-checkout. These kiosks are completely automated, through which you scan your own groceries and then bring the receipt to the cashier specific to this area of the store to pay (and some stores even offer credit and debit card usage for payment, eliminating the need for the cashier at all). Even if you use a standard checkout, the simple act of bagging your own groceries can speed up the process and often guarantees that those eggs don't end up getting crushed by a family-sized can of tomatoes placed there by a disinterested teenager or mentally inept worker.

Some grocery chains are starting to offer online grocery shopping. If you know what you want (and preparation will be a constant theme in this essay), you can select the items you want through their websites and then have them delivered right to your home.

Work: Though this may only apply to those Satanists who are able to take advantage of it, choosing employment (and even a career, if circumstances permit) that allows maximum freedom with minimal interaction could make the difference between enjoyable productivity and a disgruntled worker merely kept busy (or bored) by those around them. This can include starting your own business, choosing work that does not involve the public (such as certain tech-oriented jobs), and working at home.

For the nocturnal Satanist, there are overnight shift jobs that are usually harder to fill by employers due to the majority's diurnal schedules, sometimes pay better, and often don't require interaction with anyone. They are usually not very demanding in terms of effort, so the time managing Satanist may find this situation advantageous to catch up on reading, studying, or projects that can be done on paper or a laptop computer. Since these types of jobs aren't generally career material, they more often than not serve as supplemental income.

For the more career-minded of us, a dual proposition can be summarized as thus: "Is this line of work both satisfying to me *and* comparatively free of unnecessary interaction?" The notion often pounded into many in their childhood is that working with people or, perhaps more to the point, forced cooperative situations are universal in the workforce. This is limited and dualistic thinking on the parts of those who by and large cannot look outside their own artificially created confines, because they simply buy the scam and/or because of their own limited potential. Regarding the latter, Satanists are able to ferret out the Third Side alternative in employment matters when such ground is fertile for the application of Lesser Magic.

Banking: Believe it or not, some banks in the United States (and perhaps even other countries) are open on Saturdays. Many times, most people don't know this so it can be a potentially good time to do your banking. If this isn't an option, try going during the typical work hours of the majority, especially between 1 p.m. and 3 p.m. (after most lunch breaks, but well before the traditional shift end). Having all of your slips filled out at home can also expedite this errand.

If your bank has it, I highly recommend online banking. This is slowly but surely becoming a trend with many banks. Since checking accounts grant many the use of debit cards, bills can be paid electronically through either the use of those cards or with the checking account number itself. Direct deposit is an additional option, and along with the use of an online service like PayPal (www.paypal.com), you can cut bank trips down to a bare minimum, if not entirely.

Mail: For those of us who do not get their mail at home (nor trust the public availability and the potential theft opportunity that a Satanist's residential mailbox might invite), mail is often handled at the post office. With the rise of the Internet, much letter writing and general correspondence can be handled via e-mail, which can be a real aid. For all other mail needs, the occasional journey to the post office is eventual. But there are also ways to cut down on the visits.

The United States Postal Service has a website (www.usps.com), at or from which Americans can purchase stamps, print out labels, send money orders, track packages, calculate postage, etc. (Those in other countries may or may not be able to find their nation's equivalent.) Also, note the patterns in how full or empty your post office gets from day to day, time to time, and aim for that less frantic window of opportunity if the trip is necessary. In addition, consider picking up mail once or twice a week instead of every day.

Goods: Here's yet again another instance where the phrase, "Use the Internet" applies. Not only are varied discounts part of online shopping, but selection is often better, your purchases can be delivered by mail, and no lines of pointless, impolite, and/or miscellaneous humans. To some extent, even the added perk of browsing is included with such online dealers as amazon.com, who provide customers with on-screen product samplings. Other websites have followed or will follow suit in the future, current trends lending.

For larger purchases, there may still be the need for direct contact with merchandisers and product. Choose stores that lack mass appeal yet still provide what you're looking for. Since many Satanists enjoy items of a nostalgic or antiquated quality, places that sell such items are found to be far less attractive by the multitudes, who buy more for identity than stimulation. Also, Internet researching your desired material item(s) beforehand can save time and get you out quicker.

Movies: For the most part, the moviegoing experience isn't what it used to be. Virtually gone are the days of polite and quiet attendees, clean theaters, lavish decor, and well-dressed help. But, if you still have a love for that one remaining draw -- that of a movie projected onto the big screen -- try going at times when the soccer moms and barely involved dads don't drag along their irresponsible offspring. If your schedule permits, matinée shows during a weekday often result in almost empty theaters, the comparatively perfect moviewatching condition. Waiting a few weeks past a film's premiere will often make this even more of a reality.

But if the idea of the modern theater experience is simply too draining, there are many options available. Movie rentals are certainly at the top of the list. If you have a DVD player, you can avoid the chain rental stores altogether by visiting Netflix (www.netflix.com), through which you can rent DVDs of the newest titles and even some classics. Likewise, Pay-Per-View has similar benefits, and both eliminate traditional returns and late fees -- two more unnecessary trips.

So, what if you still feel that you'll miss out on movie trailers? Solutions exist for this as well. Netflix provides movie previews for many of their titles right on their website. Also, websites such as movies.com and comingsoon.net are rife with Quicktime, Windows Media Player, or Realplayer scaled-down versions of these previews. If you subscribe to your local paid or free newspaper, many of these also have reviews of films, something that is also abundant on the Internet.

Other Entertainment/Media: What sadly gets overlooked by some Satanists -- particularly younger ones who may still have a bit of popular cultural influence to shed -- is that there is a wealth of entertainment media either specifically geared towards Satanists, or falls into the category of *de facto* Satanic media from the past and present. In addition to the varied media of the past listed in the appendices of *The Church of Satan* by Blanche Barton (and added to in the Sources section of the official Church of Satan website: www.churchofsatan.com), here is a list of resources, both online and offline, which can serve as a welcomed alternative:

Online discussion: Put plainly, no Satanic online discussion areas in cyberspace (save the SIGs, mentioned later) measure up to Letters To The Devil (www.satannet.com). Access to sections of the board are stratified by non-CoS membership, CoS registered membership, and beyond -- in effect, keeping more meaningful discussions away from the general rabble, and more introductory posts for visitors, curiosity seekers, and those new to their Satanic affiliation. If collaboration with other Church of Satan members on projects and related endeavors is your aim, there is also the Church of Satan Special Interest Groups (also known as the SIGs). Access to this board is for approved Church of Satan members only, which further aids in stratification as well as focus. To request information on the SIGs, send off an e-mail to HPNadramia@churchofsatan.com.

Print/Periodicals: Satanism in the 21st Century is certainly not short on reading material. Since the publishing of official Church of Satan texts over the past few decades, an entire armada of published efforts has come forth. Magazines such as *The Black Flame*, *The Cloven Hoof*, *Not Like Most*, and others linked from the Church of Satan website's Links section are a refreshing change from many mainstream publications whose only apparent purpose seems to be regurgitating popular sentiments and impersonal concepts. Also, check out Purging Talon's other book releases (that is, in addition to the one you are reading now) at www.purgingtalon.com as well as the selection at Scapegoat Publishing's website, found at www.scapegoatpublishing.com.

Music and Art: There are quite a number of talented artists and musicians in Satanism whose evocative works represent both our aesthetic and our chosen alienation from the trends and derivation rampant in much of modern populist media. Many of these artists and musicians should be linked from the Church of Satan website. Keep an eye out on that same website for CoS-approved interviews, podcasts, and various Internet radio endeavors as well, often reported on in their News section.

As with all media, whether or not it has the "S" word attached to it, individual discrimination is key to any real enjoyment. It's never a case of there being a lack of choices but some will require actual effort to find.

Environment: This entire subject has been adequately covered by Dr. LaVey in his many writings and quotations. Select readings include:

> *Satan Speaks!*: "Entertain Me", "Acquisition", "Sound Retreat", "What's New", "Total Environments: Some Further Suggestions"

> *The Devil's Notebook*: "The Merits of Artificiality", "The Construction of Artificial Human Companions", "Misanthropia"

> *The Secret Life of a Satanist*: "The Humanoids Are Coming"

Attire: As a public form of the Total Environment concept, the well-crafting of dress for both aesthetic and pragmatic purposes can easily discourage unnecessary human interaction. Instead of choosing modes of clothing that will predictably elicit, say, negative reaction from the masses (such as many subculture uniforms do), try donning a wardrobe that is both appealing to you and inconsequential to the herd. By keeping this in mind, the Satanist can directly avoid the entire fashion show mentality pervasive in modern culture by simply opting out of it.

Speech: You'd be surprised just how many undesirable people will gravitate to you by clinging to a common use of popular language. The implication is that, by often sporting overtly-used slang, phrases, and adages, you appear accessible. Avoiding this requires diminishing or totally preventing that opportunity. At the fore of this utilization of language is the eradication of terminology which expresses herd value judgments. Pay attention to your own speech, and see if the words you use convey a majority opinion instead of your own. If so, weeding them out will slowly but surely disallow unwanted accessibility.

With many of these options (and the previous two in particular), it all becomes a matter of priority. Just how important concepts such as privacy, chosen intimacies, and the avoidance of mediocrity and time wasters are in the face of dealing with the dominant culture needs to be weighed in order to achieve maximum enjoyment of your life.

While the masses are evidently fine with being fed their entertainment, values, and world views unquestioningly, we Satanists must ask the whys and wherefores -- especially when our cherished and mindful isolation is threatened.

THE INTERNET: TOOL OF STRATIFICATION

As both a shrewd businessman and a calculating self-promoter, I recognize the Internet as a marvelously engineered tool that, compared to previous means, eliminates extra costs, speeds up exposure time, and gets to a bigger and wider audience than ever before. By extension, I can position both myself and my work for maximum benefit by exploiting all available avenues along the Information Superhighway. For those of us who rode the zine publishing craze of the 1990s yet survived it when it died, the Internet was the likely reason. And being in a sustainable niche market didn't hurt, either.

For the grand majority of netizens, the Internet began in 1993, even if some didn't get online for a number of years after that. Much of that late-coming probably has to do with not knowing such a virtual arena existed then, let alone knowing it came with pictures -- dirty ones, if you're diligent enough. And, there are still those who aren't online, due to age, lack of desire, or living in an area that doesn't even have phone service, let alone an available ISP. And I can't even imagine the sheer number of people who haven't the slightest idea what such terms as FTP, USENET, podcasting, or RSS mean. So, the Internet is, relatively speaking, still in its infancy for most. However, not for me. I have a markedly different tale to tell.

I have been consistently online since 1984 -- back when I was known as 74627.1020 (a now-useless CompuServe ID number burned forever in my mind). Yes, you read that correctly: 1984. That Orwellian year that never was marked my foray into cyberspace, and although some of you never knew that the Internet was around in the 1980s (its roots go back to the 1960s, actually), let alone remember what stage of development it was in, allow me to elaborate. It was glorious! Well, okay, it had its perks *and* drawbacks, like many things that are now old or "outdated."

Of course, trying to explain the Internet to anyone in the 1980s was only slightly easier than solving the Rubik's Cube blindfolded and without cheating by disassembly/reassembly. I got it. Matthew Broderick in the movie, *WarGames* got it. Tron *really* got it! But other people simply didn't get it, nor could they understand its appeal. "You mean, you talk to computers? No, wait, you type things on the screen and other people type back? That's wicked gay, dude!" And, this, ladies and gentleman, is about as insightful and intelligent as most folks got when, like deer caught in headlights, they received their first exposure of the online world that I'd given them. I suppose it took pretty graphics and the media to convince the stragglers. Now, those "stupid" message boards and chat rooms (as well as their offspring) are pretty much the totality of the Net for a great number of people. Maybe some of those users are the kids of the naysayers I knew back then, gleefully chiding their parents for their lack of computer skills. Wait... is *that* "revenge of the nerds?" Eureka! It finally came!

So, in 1984, I had e-mail (and, of course, no one to send e-mail to until the mid-1990s), chat rooms, message boards, online content, reviews, movie listings, online gaming, etc. But, before you start assuming relative similarities between online then and online now, it would be fair to say that it was, in many respects, a different animal. For the most part, the Internet didn't come with pictures, icons, dialog boxes, or any non-character display. In fact, it was all Command Line Interface, meaning that you navigated solely by text entries. I think I even have my CompuServe book from back then with an entire reference section containing hundreds of "GO" commands I'd type in to access the various areas of the service. And not a mouse in sight.

While still trapped in the land of ASCII, CompuServe wasn't exactly the prettiest gal on the block but she was the only one putting out and that made her rather special. (For perspective, I was one of 4000 people who was commercially online in 1984. That changes the quality of communication pretty sharply when contrasted against the millions of wildly random users now.)

There really was an exclusivity element to the Internet back then. I'd even go so far as to say that such exclusivity was a reasonable part of its charm and draw for me, though that would be in terms of utility and *not* identity. Since practically no one knew it existed, it was like a secret place, a cabal of shut-ins, nerds, whiz kids, business people, tech geeks, and other folks shunned for being too brainy or odd. As a result, the conversation level on message boards and in chat rooms was, a huge amount of the time, incredibly stimulating, real, educational, and by and large more engaging than the fashion victims and sports-obsessed no-minds I had to share space with five days a week in high school. It was intellectual bliss. Hard to say that about the whole of the Internet now, isn't it?

Yes, things changed come 1992-1993. The World Wide Web was now available to the public, ISPs were offering better deals (as well as actually advertising now), and a deluge of content surfaced as a result of public interest and participation. Commercial ISPs were now accessible via GUI instead of the old CLI and its all-text navigation -- spurred by the rise of Mac OS and Windows, and the reason why we even have the Web in its present visual form in the first place. In many ways, all of these developments really improved the Internet: the sheer amount of information (both credible and contestable) buries the old days hands down. But, the flipside of that, and what is markedly different from the pre-1993 years, is the enormous flood of juvenilia, psychosis, propaganda, misdirected anger, and a hodge-podge of life complaints from those who now have the voice no one else would (or even wanted to) grant them. Still, where was all of this online porn when I was 13?

In present day, the ubiquity of the Internet has altered the playing field considerably. Now, everyone gets a turn. And because of this, many users have taken interaction to an extremely casual level across the board (even with complete strangers), dispensing with an otherwise expected level of formality or even caution. As a byproduct of being reduced to screen names and avatars, the multitudes pick up the loathsome habit of assuming familiarity where none really exists, and then bring that into the real world. Give monkeys technology -- Internet, cell phones, laptops -- and they'll end up scraping their rectums out with it. Somewhere in a college library, there's an over-coddled kid writing his mid-term paper in Internet shorthand slang. "Hey, d00d, lik3, sc1enc3 i5 k00L n shizzle. LOL."

The Internet has also helped along our already convenience-based culture. The same people who want DVD players on their SUV dashboards and remote controls for their iPods are also the people who can't be bothered with using titles, last names, or any form of courtesy... that would take actual effort. They want life to come with Cliffs Notes. And forget respect. They want entitlement with no argument. And woe to you if you hurt the current generation's often oversensitive feelings cultivated by their smothering and overindulgent parents. Even in high school, I knew an obscene number of them would raise weak kids. Seems I should have bet money on it.

I'm not against the mass consumerism aspect of this, mind you. Mencken summarized my position on that best: "No one in this world, so far as I know, has ever lost money by underestimating the intelligence of the great masses of the plain people." Yes, they are, by and large, brainless monkeys with bank accounts. The youth attraction to the ever-pathetic ghetto trash culture alone is telling in this regard. And while people doing what the media tells them to do is nothing new, it now rides side-saddle with this rapidly homogenizing and convenience-expecting paradigm. "We're ALL okay, we're ALL the same, we should ALL get the same things" ...blah, blah, blah, *ad nauseam*.

I once thought that the medium might actually get people more practiced in their language through more frequent communication. Boy, was that dangerously optimistic. Again, it's like leading horses to water, trying to teach pigs to sing, etc. But, it's not the Internet alone. In fact, it couldn't be. It takes a foundation to build that house upon, and its name is egalitarianism.

It's the very reason why the herd love the Internet -- because, once online, they leave (or believe that they leave) their insecurities, fears, and ineptitude behind and become one amongst faceless millions. It mirrors the most nauseating aspects of democracy (read: politicized Judeo-Christianity), making sure everyone feels like they matter despite merit or level of ability or intelligence.

And while they're reinventing themselves behind the safety of a keyboard, they can also make "friends." The Internet is rife with opportunities for desperate approval and bonding between otherwise socially inept people. One night at a local bar, I actually overheard some girl literally begging her partymates to join her MySpace page so she could "get more numbers" in her displayed list of friends. Such candor! And it turns out this isn't an isolated occurrence as I've also run into this similarly worded desire *way* too many times now on websites, blogs, message boards, and newsgroups -- user after user obsessed with getting people (anyone, really) to join their MySpace pages to increase the appearance of "friends" therein. What miserable lives some of them must have. Tell me they're getting something besides empty praise out of the deal. Or are they even getting that!?

One encompassing point that a lot of this makes, for me, is that the concept of friends really means very little to many people. And it doesn't take a social networking website to point that out, as evidence for this practice is everywhere and seemingly more rampant than previous decades. Maybe there is a depersonalization factor to the Internet that aids in trivializing all relationships for certain types of people. Or maybe the Internet is a shoddy excuse for the shallow to justify their lack of interpersonal relationship skills. In any case, disposable (or even mischanneled) relationships will probably always be a part of our individual cultures. And technology might often be involved.

And I'm no technophobe, by any means. Nor do I wish technology to be characterized as a scapegoat. But it seems that 21st century humans in tech-driven cultures have a really difficult time getting together and having a one-on-one, face-to-face conversation while, in marked contrast, they are at times eerily over-reliant upon chat rooms, message boards, Instant Messaging, e-mail, cell phones (!), text messaging, etc. Even still, I'm not as curious about why people make these choices as I am about what the outcome of these choices will be. Call me practical.

I suppose that if folks are going to desperately hurl themselves to the masses, beg for acceptance, and then place some sort of stock in their fake relationships, it should at least be entertaining. How about some unintentionally revealing self-hatred poetry, or maybe a nervous breakdown via webcam, or perhaps even a "final post" before logging off... for good. The spotlight's on them. In fact, they placed it there, so they may as well put on the full song and dance for the rest of us.

Of course in the online world, fools come in all stripes and some of them are certainly attracted to Satanism, or at least what they think it is. Yes, their knowledge on the subject runs the gamut: from music subculture idiots to those who want to rewrite Satanism for their own lame purposes, and still many unimaginative others. In all cases, it's clear (though, sometimes not to them) that they are grossly incompatible with Satanism but their fragile egos can't handle the rejection. So, they whine and fuss and throw their best hissy fits in misguided dissent, blubbering that the Church of Satan made a mistake in sending them on their way or that (all of a sudden) we're not practicing *real* Satanism -- a conclusion many didn't manage to reach until the most convenient moment for it, of course. Methinks they protest too late.

The Internet enters the picture when the recently rejected, or non-Satanist in denial, finds that there are other rejects online who also had their membership fees turned away as a result of criminal activity and other well-advertised stupidity on the Web, or figured out slowly that what is and always has been firmly established Satanic philosophy runs counter to their own personalities and dispositions. Seeing as some simply can't take no for an answer, a vocal minority of them band together, forming their sob-sister "organizations" by setting up terribly designed websites, even *more* terribly designed MySpace pages (complete with a confused mish-mash of stolen graphics, photos, and videos, often pilfered from the sites of legitimate CoS members), and maybe even actual message boards, all to endlessly bitch and moan like spurned lovers about the fascist, tyrannical, nefarious (and don't forget elitist) CoS and how it's all changed since Dr. LaVey died.

The truth is that it hasn't. And when put to brass tacks, all of their accusations come up predictably empty in the specificity department. None of them have any clear, factual, and substantial explanations for how the Church of Satan has steered away from the foundation laid down by LaVey, other than those complaints deeply rooted in their own (or someone else's) illiterate misunderstandings of *The Satanic Bible*. In most cases, they are on the outside looking in, and it embarrassingly shows in their assertions. But still undeterred, a dozen voices will cry in white trash unison, "It's just changed, man!" Okay... man. Tell it to the ragtag flock of drug-addled teens, subculture losers, petty criminals, disturbed sluts, abused kids, and various throwaways that you've managed to attract. Because Christians need their Devil just like pseudo-Satanists need the Church of Satan. I think I speak for all of us when I say that you can have the wastrels. You can be a filter for stratification. Job's all yours. Thanks for playing.

Of course, the primary stratification filter is the Internet itself. Before all of this, a Satanic hopeful or even a longtime card-carrying member might have never discovered any conflict between himself and the philosophy. He could have gone on his merry way, safe in the ignorance of quasi-understanding *The Satanic Bible* at best and thinking he's a very powerful and erudite Satanist because nothing or no one is seemingly available to prove otherwise. But thanks to the Internet, he is now exposed to very real Satanists -- to our work, our ideas and thoughts, our modes of behavior -- and that doesn't allow him to kid himself for very long by comparison. He must contend with actual Satanists from around the world who not only read TSB far more carefully than he did, but are also living examples of it. At this moment, the bubble has been burst.

And that exposure runs both ways. Rather than make a quiet exit, some of these receivers of rude awakening loudly exclaim their position all over the Internet, but with generous amounts of over-dramatic spin. Some attempt to make trouble, while others just demand to be listened to by anyone who won't make fun of them. In short, they red-flag themselves -- often, unknowingly. And we all have this marvelous technology to thank. So, thank you, Internet. Please continue to provide rope to the hang-worthy.

So, sure, the Internet isn't what it used to be and, in some ways, I'm glad it isn't. I certainly don't miss the original $6 (night rate) or $12 (day rate) an hour connect time charges from the early days (and that's in 1980s money). If anything, you can even *make* money from all of this nonsense, if you play your cards right. All in all, it's a bigger and sometimes better beast than before, even if there's now a morass of muck to wade through. And, there are ways to streamline your online interactions while denying the direct moronic prattle of over-stimulated brats and under-educated hayseeds who "just gots their new 'puter." Where are those obscured corners of cyberspace, you ask? That's for you to find out.

From Out Of The Woodwork

Over the past 20+ years that I have rightfully taken the title of Satanist, I've seen myriad strains of the Satanic hopeful: the church-desecrating metalheads, the Satanic groupie gals, the '90s breed of rockstar-driven Satanic dabblers, those hiding under contrived horns to mask insecurity or ineptitude, you name it (and trust me when I say that as a result of being a member of the Priesthood of the Church of Satan, I have run into my share of ass-kissers of both genders with the obvious agenda of currying favor from an official of the CoS, so throw them into the pot as well). Some of them align with the Church of Satan temporarily, all to predictably fall away after an embarrassingly long period of time when they finally get it through their heads that they are not one of us. Others (which include some from the previous sentence) form their own little "Satanic" groups of which, again, dissolve into nothingness to a reliable degree of certainty. Usually, these people are as transparent as they come and merit little mention more than this paragraph requires. Establishing that, there remains one other type of Satanic aspirant, and you might be one of them!

The problem generally lies in their overall understanding of Satanism, and this lack of understanding can be further divided into two camps: the Unable and the Unwilling.

The Unable are, often enough, teenagers or even uneducated adults who discover Satanism through whatever popular cultural medium is closest to them (and this includes the Internet), and upon reading some of our material and personally favorable parts of *The Satanic Bible*, instantly claim citizenship in the Infernal Empire, membership -- or even, reality -- be damned. They put on the black attire, buy a shiny, new Baphomet necklace, and bathe themselves in an exterior that, for them, paves over some normally consuming void in their lives. Luckily, the Unable don't last very long in Satanism, many times because of compelling drug addictions, overwhelming life failures, maturation beyond their fetishizing of Satanism, and sometimes, they meander off into Christian pastures where many of them, in a default sense, belong. Sometimes, nature provides its own filtration process.

The Unwilling, however, are a stickier situation. These individuals (and I use that term loosely) can be die-hard Church of Satan supporters or even members. They've feverishly gobbled up *every* single bit of media ever produced by or focused upon Anton LaVey and many of us more prominent officials and administrators of our organization -- and I mean to an obsessive collector's degree. They tend to show up on many online centers of assumed Satanic activity such as chat rooms and message boards, and with an alarming frequency. If there were such a thing as Satanic conventions, they'd surely attend them in droves. It's groupie-ism taken to its absurd limit.

Don't be fooled. Many of the Unwilling are doing all of this and more because they are practicing their craft at erroneous assimilation with the Satanic ideal -- sometimes to such a degree that even they (un?)consciously buy into their own scam. Never mind that Satanists are born and not made. These people patently ignore that reality and don the wolf's clothing to -- often, in vain -- attempt to deceive the real wolves, or, again, even themselves.

One way to ferret out any potential infestation of these pests is to ignore their pandering to our philosophy in word and study what comes in deed. In other words, the Unwilling are sometimes able to talk a good game but invariably slip up merely by defaulting to their own everyday lives. If we say personal mastery and they can't excel at anything at all; if we say ego-fulfillment and they hate themselves; if we say self-deification and they're into self-mutilation and wallowing in psychosis; if we say fierce individuality and their individual histories paint a portrait of someone massively and unpragmatically entrenched in collectivism -- all of this is evidence to the contrary of Satanic compatibility. They may even be the last to know.

Regardless, both the Unable and the Unwilling often avoid recognizing a prime criterion of Satanism and, in an attempt for balance, overcompensate in a number of others. I could care less how successful and innately intelligent you are if you can't even solve your own harmful personal problems. It charms me not that you've managed to sidestep indoctrination of popular culture if you possess no talent, insight, or intellect. You're the barely charming idiot, the attractive headcase, the talented bore -- all the while expecting me and other actual Satanists to take you seriously. Believe me when I say that your very existence speaks much more truth than your mouth ever could.

To partially summarize, the Unable skip the "big words" in *The Satanic Bible*. The Unwilling latch onto them for desperate self-validation.

But in order to maintain their illusion, they have to do what it takes -- either that or face the horror that is themselves. The one unshakable fact in the face of their elaborate (or not so elaborate) ruse is that Satanism itself rejects them outright at its most philosophical core. Unlike other religions, which accept a glut of lost, dependent, troubled, and weak-minded fools indiscriminately, Satanism has well-defined standards and qualities, some of which unattainable through environmental means yet ones with which many faux Satanists find useful in puffing themselves up beyond reality. An archetype of Will, complexity of mind, prideful alienation, and mindful rebellion, although congruent with the Satanist, could also appear attractive to those who wish to artificially reinvent themselves to gain some sort of acceptance (largely, from the Church of Satan) or "self-esteem," or simply to fulfill a daddy fixation through some perceived paternal quality in the archetype of Satan. The true Satanist needs no such self-validation, all along possessing Satanic qualities foreign to such insecurity and lack of self-driven identity.

Coming full circle, a minority of these wannabes, not content with putting themselves in a position by which they would ultimately be rejected and then have to accept blame for their own lack of discernment, feel it necessary to blame the Church of Satan for their own gross oversight, that we aren't "real" Satanism (read: something to which they can no longer attach themselves) and that they have the pure version. (This dynamic is further illustrated in the document, The Satanic Bunco Sheet, available at churchofsatan.com.) So, off they go to form their single-digit memberships (often, that number is one) to their website "church" and work themselves through their final step out of anything even remotely related to Satanism and back into the herd of which they've always been a part -- with or without the window dressing.

So, to those exploring Satanism as a potentially reflective philosophy, I would suggest actually paying attention to what the philosophy states *and* implies -- particularly before committing yourself to an inaccurate label at the expense of your credibility. I would also suggest not being an idiot, but, evidence lending, that's far too tall an order to be requested by even the Alien Elite.

SIFTING THE ASHES OF ANTON LaVEY

Since the unfortunate death of our founding High Priest in 1997, the human parasites have surfaced in full force, rolling gleefully in their own dung over whatever "hard evidence" and "insight" they can scrape together in order to fool themselves and gullible others into thinking that, this time, it will mean the end of the Church of Satan. Be they third-rate power-grabbers or loudmouth cowards (usually both), they spend far too much time, effort, and Internet bandwidth lambasting the very organization they claim is so dead. As pathetic and telling as those motives are...

Oh, hear the blames:

"Anton was never a lion tamer and he never slept with Marilyn Monroe. I know a person who has a sister who has a friend in the Temple of Set who knows someone with an Internet account who knows Ferris Bueller who has 'chatted' through the Web with some journalist who wrote that he made it all up. After all, if it makes LaVey look bad, it simply *must* be true! And it's common knowledge that all journalists are very ethical and honest professionals."

"Don't you know? The Church of Satan is no more. Yeah, it's bankrupt and is now a figment of everyone's imagination. What fools those so-called priests and magisters are that they don't see Rome falling before them. I know because I heard about some court papers out there on the Internet that say so, though I haven't seen them yet. This is *so* juicy. Just like my favorite sitcom."

"The Church of Satan is full of Nietzsche-lovin' Nazis... like that Roy

Brice guy [true identity withheld]. He's a racist, white supremacist because I saw him in a photograph wearing a swastika, and that's *proof*. If you don't believe that you can judge a book by its cover, you're a Nazi, too! Oh, yeah, and screw the CoS!" [wipes nose with shirt sleeve]

You get the point. But be amazed at the number of people who won't get the point or see the sarcasm in the previous three paragraphs. Collectively, these are an encapsulated idea of what small minds can occupy their overabundance of time with. But, since LaVey's death, there has been a visible and very suspicious increase of LaVey-detractors. How convenient that we see so many *now*. But, in light of the simian behavior that has resulted from it, how even more embarrassing.

It's one thing to dislike something; it's another to fixate on it and spend generous amounts of time and effort to "save the world" from such "evil and deceptive villains." (Those quotes are my representations of what the average LaVeyophile-in-denial might say, even if he doesn't have a Mr. Spock hairdo and worship an anteater.) Funny, but last I checked, "saving" people was the task of insecure Christians. Think it can't get any more transparent?

Well, not only do the jealous and the lonely want to save you (and save you for themselves, by the way), but they will risk their very credibility to do it. Case in point is the stale argument that LaVey's life is heavily fabricated. Why does it matter either way? Whether or not LaVey's conquest list includes a couple of famous bombshells is about as relevant to my life as what color my neighbor's urine is. Concerning yourself with specifically why LaVey's youngest daughter is so unfond of her late father is not only none of your business, but pathetic and un-Satanic. If it was still standing, I'm sure these two-bit snoops would be the first to creep around the yard of the Black House and write us a detailed Usenet posting on what color the drapes are or if that roof ever got re-shingled. Enquiring dimwits need to know these things, apparently.

And, if any of those sour-grapers are going to criticize any written account on Herr Doktor by either the man himself or Blanche Barton, why isn't that scrutiny also pointed towards these complainers? If we're going to point fingers, let's have a really asinine, aimless, and unyielding accusation-fest: Are LaVey and Barton the liars? Are certain media making facts up? Is everyone lying a little? Are we believing whatever supports our argument here? And then, in the face of it all, just how crucial is all of this? You know that one mention of "What if

LaVey faked his own death?" would keep the scavengers well busy up until their Internet bills cut into their beer money. Imagine picking up the *Weekly World News* and seeing some "Ipsissimus" waving a photo of some bald guy on a donkey in Mexico, exclaiming in a caption balloon, "I sighted LaVey" (perhaps spurring numerous "LaVey sightings" which would, to the chagrin of his self-assumed enemies, merely elevate him to true urban legend status and further into cultural iconography). Come to think of it, I may not be entirely opposed to the idea of indirectly starting this "sightings" craze myself.

But aside from this freak, tabloid occurrence, could the bickering, nit-picking, and combing through dirty laundry be that productive? I'll help out with this one: it isn't. LaVey-bashing has become a substitute for achieving real success and advanced thinking for a transparent minority. For others, the behavior helps some could-have-beens and never-will-bes appear as self-inflated big-shots; perhaps, to siphon off (pre- or post-mortem) some of LaVey's celebrity or human triumph. And, for others, it shows that they just can't accept a Satanism that isn't nice and sweet and libertarian and left-wing (or any wing, or that matter), so it's open season for *ad hominem* attacks, the only attacks they know or remember from fourth grade recess. The difference is that children don't often buy their own claptrap.

Ultimately, if parts of the personal history of Anton LaVey are fiction, then at least it's worth reading, which is more than I'll say for the accounts of the dull and uninspired blockheads who are emotionally locked onto their so-called nemesis. The Italians have an apropos expression here: *Se non é vero, é ben trovato*, or (approximately) "Even if it's not true, it's still a good story." I agree. But, more importantly, I don't need the story to be either. I will still live my life Satanically, and I will seek excellence and pleasure for the many years I have ahead.

ROSEMARY REVISITED
A SATANIC LOOK AT ONE OF THE SCARIEST MOVIES OF ALL TIME

It's likely you've seen *Rosemary's Baby* more times than you can count. You probably even know some choice lines of dialogue ("Typhoon!"), and can recite them at the drop of a hat. Maybe you've passed by the Dakota building in New York City, wondering if the Trench sisters are still chewing... something. Okay, maybe you're not *that* obsessed with the film, but it's definitely a classic -- especially to Satanists.

But, is it even possible that some of you have not seen this fine motion picture? If not, then let's bring you deprived and incomplete readers up to speed on what I'm talking about. (I will also be paying attention to the novel as well as the film, seeing as both are deserving of sizable accolades.)

Rosemary's Baby finds our two lead characters, Rosemary and Guy Woodhouse, embroiled in what slowly reveals itself to be a Satanic conspiracy to bring the son of Satan into the world of flesh. However, Rosemary is on the unknowing end of this plot, and it is her increasing discovery of these occult doings that sets the stage for the two hours and 14 minutes of this celluloid adaptation.

The story's epicenter lies underneath a foreboding apartment house on Central Park West referred to in both the novel and the film as "Black Bramford" (or, what would, by an unnamed movie reviewer, be called "Branford," one of the many errors film critics would make in their published opinions of this Roman Polanski-directed and screen-written effort) (*Time* 84). The Bramford itself adds a tenebrous aura to the developing plot with its dark, skinny corridors and exhaustively tall, Victorian ceilings, almost to the point of the building becoming an actual character.

The appearance of the apartment does not go unnoticed, least of all to Rosemary. Soon after Rosemary and Guy move into their new home, she proceeds to have the apartment painted white, perhaps an unconscious residential exorcism to wipe away the Bramford's historical residue: the lingering ghosts of two child-murdering/ cannibalistic elderly women and a cult leader's sanguinary activities and subsequent death. The *de facto* sterilization of the Woodhouse apartment is starkly contrasted to the less homogenized atmosphere of the apartment belonging to the old couple they soon meet.

These neighbors, Minnie and Roman Castavet, are a quirky and flamboyant pair who, as it turns out, are also the leaders of a Satanic coven, and who not only help Guy's floundering acting career via their devotion to the Devil, but also convince him to aid them in borrowing Rosemary's womb for the conception and birth of Satan's son. But, not without a fight from Rosemary. (As a side note, Ruth Gordon won an Oscar for her portrayal of Minnie, the only person involved with *Rosemary's Baby* to be awarded.)

As the plot evolves, Rosemary takes steps to protect her baby from the coven, a baby she assumes to be a future blood offering to the Devil and not the partial by-product of diabolical genetics. Much like the symbolic painting of the apartment, all of Rosemary's efforts to escape the reach of the Devil and his acolytes are in vain: formerly trusted people prove to be part of the coven, while others die unexplainable deaths or are cursed.

The baby is born and kept by the coven, unbeknownst to Rosemary, who is told that her child died during the birthing process. After numerous incidents of hearing a distant baby crying, Rosemary decides to investigate. With knife in hand, she passes through a secret passageway connecting her apartment to the Castavets' and stumbles upon the real conspiracy: that the coven didn't want to kill the child, but rather to praise and celebrate his existence. This concept, along with some presumedly obscure references, was hardly coincidental.

Purportedly playing the extremely brief part of the Devil as well as being an uncredited "technical advisor" for the film, was none other than Anton Szandor LaVey, High Priest and founder of the Church of Satan. LaVey reflects on what happened at the movie theater in which he and others saw the film: "People got very angry -- stomping their feet and showing general disapproval. Sometimes the reality of Satanism is a lot more terrifying to people than their safe fantasies of what it's supposed to be. For the first time they've been confronted with a Devil who talks back" (*Barton* 24). In essence, moviegoers didn't get the predictable "good triumphs over evil" ending -- the coven succeeds in their goal, and the movie ends with Rosemary tacitly accepting her child and the circumstances, with almost a hint of pleasure on her face. Perhaps this is the true terror of *Rosemary's Baby* and why this film remains as one of the most terrifying horror movies of all time: the supposed "bad guys" actually win in a film for a change.

LaVey's influence on this film appears in subtle forms as well. The son of Satan, according to both Ira Levin's book (which, by the summer of 1968, had sold 2.3 million copies) and Polanski's film, is born in 1966, which is also the year that LaVey announced the formation of the Church of Satan, one year previous to Levin's penning of the story. (This highly suggests that Levin had researched or was aware of LaVey's high media presence in the mid- to late-Sixties.) In an earlier scene in the movie (and also appearing in the novel), Roman Castavet, at a New Year's party, proudly exclaims "To 1966, the Year One." Though many movie critics at the time felt that this specifically parodied the use of "Anno Domini" in reference to a year following the birth of Christ, this was an erroneous assumption. Within the Church of Satan, 1966 is specifically called "The Year One" in tribute to the Church's year of inception; again, this is one year previous to Levin's novel. For the initiated, this may have also attributed to the film's suspense, or served as a humorous Satanic in-joke.

And, judging from Polanski's previous efforts (which include *Repulsion*, *Cul-de-sac* and *The Fearless Vampire Killers*), suspense seemed a reliable addition for this motion picture. This may explain why he removed a specific scene in Levin's book: when Rosemary left the city and spent some time alone in a cabin in the woods to evaluate her situation. In terms of pacing, this scene would have also allowed the viewers time to contemplate, enough to relax and, hence, release the tension that Polanski struggled so hard to instill. This, at an advanced moment in the plot where such a pause would be awkward and, perhaps, disastrous.

Excluding the omitted scene, Levin's novel practically reads like the script to the movie, almost as if he envisioned his story to evolve to the Big Screen. The text is largely in dialogue form and, subsequently, easily translatable to the film medium. This is telling as Levin has had many of his books turned into adaptations including *The Stepford Wives* (1975), *The Boys From Brazil* (1978), and *Sliver* (1993), to name a few.

This strongly implies that Levin might write with a vision of a motion picture to follow, in turn, making Polanski's job that much easier.

Since Polanski did use the book in a largely verbatim sense, this is much of the reason why the first half of the film comes under scrutiny. At least one critic at the time felt this half to be ineffective, referring to it as "the cumbersome building-block method" that wasn't as effective as the saving grace of the last half (*Kauffmann* 26). The first half does indeed move slowly: many scenes of Rosemary and Guy's daily life, decorating the apartment, discussing careers, having dinner with the neighbors and other seemingly mundane matters. It is my contention that this is necessary for character and plot development. In order for the story to work, the viewer must care about the characters, and this doesn't come by thrusting stock figures into a scary script, unless you're attempting to make another *Friday the 13th* or Temple of Set. The terror in this film is beyond such ham-handed and product-oriented tactics. *Rosemary's Baby* shuns the now-cliché hack-and-slash game in favor of psychological warfare. Perhaps unintentionally, it would be this film that would spawn a barrage of cinematic gorefests throughout the 1970s and, most notably, the 1980s.

And, with few exceptions, many of these 90-minute bloodbaths have been relegated to the bargain bin at video stores while *Rosemary's Baby* remains a classic. I would say that the longevity of Polanski's masterpiece lies in the immutable reality that visual shock value cannot adequately compete on equal ground with psychological tinkering. For example, it is one thing to show an audience footage of the dead bodies of Nazi concentration camp victims; it is another to ponder the ideology behind the extermination of an entire group of people. To know that the latter has greater impact in the long run is to understand the intelligent effects of this film.

One fairly revealing item from Levin's novel that Polanski not only includes but makes reference to more than once is the Pope's visit to New York that actually occurred in real life during the time that Rosemary conceives her child in the story. Levin thought it would be an intriguing contrast and add to the drama. During the ritual/ impregnation scene (which does appear in the book), Rosemary asks for absolution from a Pope-like figure and receives it. It is interesting to note that during this time, Anton LaVey was referred to by the media and others as "the Black Pope."

But, like many things in life, this film isn't perfect. Though the presence of Rosemary's dream sequences was explained in Levin's book, Polanski's version of these sequences was vague, surreal, and bordering on drug-imagery: trends in '60s filmmaking, influenced by a subculture that Polanski was intimately familiar with. While these scenes may have sparked some fascination with select audience members at that time, they appear as visual masturbation and almost schizophrenic to the modern breed of moviegoer.

And the critics are somewhat correct about the non-Rosemary characters being a bit less important. Somewhat correct. True, the story is about Rosemary and her baby (if it wasn't, it would probably be called something else), but I see most of the other characters as more than just stock. Roman and Minnie carry a great sympathy and sweetness (read: Lesser Magic) only the aged can deliver, and the more this is played up, the more startling (for the non-Satanists, anyway) the news of them being consorts of the Devil really is. Guy, Rosemary's husband, is consistently portrayed as a bad actor (as opposed to John Cassavetes being a bad actor, which in this production, he wasn't). The well-crafted revealing of Guy being both an unsuccessful actor onstage and an equally bad liar to Rosemary offstage is balanced deftly, and took a convincing performance from Cassavetes to make it believable.

However, the critics are dead on the mark concerning less than memorable performances from Ralph Bellamy as the conspiring obstetrician, Dr. Saperstein, as well as that from Maurice Evans as Rosemary's shortly-lived confidant, Hutch. These characters were necessary but could have been played by actors half as competent as the aforementioned two without damaging the story. Even more so, all other characters could have been delivered by less experienced actors, perhaps even extras.

Considering that the novel and film are in many ways similar, I'd argue that the latter is superior, but not by a landslide. The omission of the cabin scene found in the book, Polanski's experience with the genre, the appropriate use of music (brilliantly and, to some extent, innovatively composed by Christopher Komeda, known for providing the soundtracks to many of Polanski's films), while remaining sizably faithful to Levin's vision bring the film version barely above its literary predecessor. Polanski also keeps alive the spirit of the original in the sense of its subterfuge: that current of iniquity and decadence flowing underneath a mantle of charm, respectability and grace which Levin aptly directs in his book.

Perhaps the ultimate conclusion is that Rosemary's Baby shows us both sides of the human coin, that we are both benevolent and brutal, and that these forces are indivisible, no matter how many dualistic labels and religious sun-fearing people deceitfully subscribe to. When all other fun fear is shed, the deepest layer of terror is the realization of human nature.

Works Cited

Barton, Blanche. *The Church of Satan*. New York: Hell's Kitchen. 1990.

Kauffmann, Stanley. "Son of a Witch." *New Republic* 15 Jun. 1968: 26.

Levin, Ira. *Rosemary's Baby*. Greenwich, CT: Fawcett Crest. 1967.

"Rosemary's Baby." *Time* 21 Jun. 1968: 84.

Rosemary's Baby. Dir. Roman Polanski. Perf. Mia Farrow, John Cassavetes, and Ruth Gordon. Paramount, 1968.

B-HORROR DATES TO DISMEMBER

[The following essay's title is a derivation of "B-Horror Etiquette" by Vanilla Christ, appearing in *Poo Poo Magazine* #14. This piece was both inspired by its elder and serves as a continuation of an exploration into its respective movie genre]

The last twenty years (1977-1997) have procured some of the best (and, admittedly, the campiest) slasher films to date, both establishing the man behind the hockey mask's bogeyman icon and magnifying the very real depravity behind the eyes of our Ted Bundys and Jeffrey Dahmers. These movies say a lot about us as a culture and a species of life; perhaps, more than most upstanding or politically-correct citizens would want to admit. They are the progeny of our collective psyche, our secret desire/repulsion capacity, and they certainly serve as a pathway to our occasionally repressed need for eustress.

But, while few remember the date that Charming Ted was executed, millions recall the day Jason presides over, or the night Michael Meyers knifed his big sister and adopted the anniversary as his eve of destruction on one small town. While the murderers on our nation's death rows are dispatched and forgotten, their cinematic equivalents are immortalized on the silver screen and in the minds of generations of slasher franchise fans.

Perhaps, a distinction lies in the safety net of the screen itself; it keeps the demons on the other side of the wall, while only hinting to the real-life, largely less colorful, and comparably less visible serial murderers of our time. If catharsis is the true religion of the masses, then horror cinema is unquestionably the blood and body which many take and ingest. From a polite distance, of course.

Hollywood knows this consumerist fact all too well, and had doubtlessly learned it well by the early-1980s. The gore merchants of Tinseltown want you to have a memorable experience. Why not attach a date or holiday to the two-dimensional carnage to secure this impression? Holidays are relatable, practically unavoidable, and contain various expectations and memories; all vulnerable to reinterpretation. Like words reused and put into a modern context, the redefining of special occasions is the stuff that gives a horror director a persistent bulge in the nether-region, figuratively speaking.

So, when you break in that new calendar next year, think of these happy, good-natured partygoers (who just happen to be carrying bloody chainsaws around with them) and all of their hard work.

Starting off the sanguine-soaked year is a chunk of celluloid entitled *New Year's Evil* (1981), a not-so-memorable auld lang syne centered around a DJ and a killer; one bit of cinema that makes an eggnog hangover seem more enjoyable (or scarier).

As February rolls in, our black hearts long for love... or the sound of power tools against flesh and bone. The Canadian-made, *My Bloody Valentine* (1981) introduces us to the blood-crazed coalminer character (fortunately, *not* a precedent setter) who terrorizes the girls and boys of Valentine Bluffs. Someone should tell this psycho that gas masks, though scary, kill peripheral vision.

But, alas, the winter thaw makes way for the Technicolor splendor of spring, but showers aren't the only thing that April brings. *April Fool's Day* (1986), with quite a bit more reservedness, somewhat succeeds at the horror-as-humor premise that *Student Bodies* hacked to pieces five years earlier. A college coed invites her collegiate pals to her family's island mansion to pull an elaborate practical joke on them: each one is sequentially "killed" off, until the end when the audience discovers that no one died! It's a joke. Get it? Do you care?

As spring flutters to a close and school prepares to let out for the summer, adolescents around the nation are preparing for the biggest night of their high school lives: Senior Prom. *Prom Night* (1980) brings Jamie Lee Curtis back to the horror world (*Terror Train*, another Curtis flick, also hit theatres in this same year) in a tale of teen revenge murder sparked in response to the unintended death of a little girl years earlier by a group of cruel children (now teenagers... can you smell the plot yet?). This film would spawn three incredibly formulaic bomb sequels, which never come close to comparing to the original (a common horror movie story).

Even dear old Mom is dragged into the fray with *Mother's Day* (1980), a cross between *I Spit On Your Grave* and *Texas Chainsaw Massacre* (though, not of the same level of fun-fear). Two misogynist hillbillies torture and kill coeds for Mama. Isn't that sweet? (On a related note, the vignette, "Father's Day" from the movie *Creepshow* is a fabulously ghoulish sketch of an old man coming back from the dead to deal out his revenge on his murderous daughter and the random estate occupant who gets in his way.)

And, just when you thought it was safe to be a summer camp counselor comes *Friday The 13th* (1980), a box office smash and the grand-daddy of psychokiller films, spawning a neverending number of imitators as well as *eight* sequels as of 1997, largely directed by a different director every film (the exception, being that Parts II and III were directed by Steve Miner). With Jason Voorhees as a household name, even television couldn't resist (judging by the short-lived TV series based on the movies... or at least their name). Horror creeps still argue exhaustively over whether Jason is "cooler" than Freddy, the child-molester/killer from the *Nightmare On Elm Street* series of films... and neither chain of movies has been made recently. That's devotion!

With the rise of the harvest moon (and the corporate world's need to sell candy and plastic costumes) comes *Halloween* (1978) and the all-too-understated killer character of Michael Meyers. This movie gave birth to five sequels as of 1997, all of declining quality and massive formulaic pap. Still, the original serves as one of the most classic horror movies in Hollywood's history (and spurs Jamie Lee Curtis into a series of hack and slash motion pictures following. See: *Prom Night*).

Wrapping up the year in fleshy ribbons and organ bows comes a cup of Christmas fear known as *Silent Night, Deadly Night* (1984). This screen opus focuses on the acted-out predilections of an axe murderer dressed in a Santa suit, and made way for four sequels. (This movie was also picketed nationwide.) But, the holiday fun doesn't stop there. *Silent Night, Bloody Night* (1973) is a delightful low-budget romp through the eyes of an insane asylum escapee / murderer's slashathon through a small New England town. And, if *that's* not enough, put out milk and cookies for *Black Christmas* (1975; also called *Silent Night, Evil Night*, and *Stranger In The House*). This last effort chronicles a killer's Christmas Eve murder spree through a sorority house. Interesting to note that the season of the most suicides also provokes an abundance of horror movies related to the holiday (and there are others on the yuletide theme, rest assured). The Grinch should be envious.

And, if you've desperately doubted that nothing is sacred, not even the anniversary of one's birth is spared. *Happy Birthday To Me* (1981) is a sad attempt at horror filmmaking with a rather ambiguous ending. Canada has served up better slasher films.

Seeing as most of these and similar films were made in the 1980s, perhaps we've seen the end of the holiday-themed horror film. Quite the letdown for those eagerly awaiting an *Arbor Day Massacre*, or the promisingly quixotic, *Terror On Flag Day*. Optimistically, the fine art of this horror breed may merely be lying dormant, waiting for the gifted to read the incantation that will resurrect its rustic, brain-damaged spirit once again. Whatever the case may be, summer camp, proms, and garden tools will never be looked at in quite the same way again.

THE SATANIC SIDE OF THE ENLIGHTENMENT

"Sometimes the reality of Satanism is a lot more terrifying to people than their safe fantasies of what it's supposed to be. For the first time, they've been confronted with a Devil that talks back."
- Anton Szandor LaVey (*The Secret Life of A Satanist*, 92)

This indeed was the case on the night of April 30th, 1966 when Anton LaVey (1930-1997) shaved his head and officially announced the founding of the San Francisco-based Church of Satan, marking the event as the "Year One." Three years later, this former lion tamer, carnival organist, police photographer, and "occult investigator" would publish his most notorious religious / philosophical tome, *The Satanic Bible*, followed by four additional books in the decades to follow. A media circus exploded at this time that would widely report the activities of this "Black Pope," from his performance of the first publicized Satanic baptism of one of his own daughters, to the weddings and funerals he'd conducted in the name of the Devil, to his purported relationships with such notables as Marilyn Monroe, Kenneth Anger, Jayne Mansfield, Sammy Davis Jr. and others. LaVey died two days before Halloween of 1997 at the age of 67. Like those influential thinkers LaVey obliquely celebrated through his writing and his lifestyle, he too had to go the way of all flesh.

And LaVey's influences were myriad: from *Frankenstein* and *Dracula* to Mark Twain and *Weird Science* comics to Nietzsche and Machiavelli. His aim to synthesize a religion based on "rational self-interest" and a "healthy ego championed" by using the archetype of Satan as the rebel, the accuser, the adversary, had not only made a sizable number of people reconsider their "privileged lies" but also exposed many to great works of philosophy (specifically, those pertaining to personal liberty) that could have otherwise drifted away in the wake of television, video games and the Internet (*The Satanic Bible*, 14). Though such works as *The Prince*, *Might Is Right*, and *The Antichrist* gain center stage as *de facto* Satanic influences, the Enlightenment period (1600s to late-1700s) may also shed some light on the Prince of Darkness's pensive side.

Early in the Enlightenment, Thomas Hobbes (1588-1679) published his treatise on the human condition, known by the rather diabolical moniker of *Leviathan*. Leviathan, in addition to being a Hebrew mythological sea monster, is also considered by Satanists as one of the Crown Princes of Hell, represented by the compass point, west. Keep in mind that Satanists speak in a largely metaphorical language and that there is no professed belief in actual anthropomorphic deities, just useful archetypes.

In *Leviathan*, Hobbes illustrates man as being in a constant state of war -- most importantly, a war of man against man. The Satanic viewpoint would parallel this sentiment as illustrated by the seventh Satanic Statement in *The Satanic Bible*:

> "Satan represents man as just another animal, sometimes better, more often worse than those that walk on all-fours, who, because of his 'divine spiritual and intellectual development,' has become the most vicious animal of all!" (25).

Hobbes further proposes in Chapter 14 of *Leviathan* that since man seeks self-preservation -- the "highest law" to the Satanist -- he develops the social contract with others in order to form a civilization and, by extension, to remain alive. It is crucial to understanding both Hobbes and LaVey that this formation is not done out of some unconditional affection for humankind or similar altruistic motives but rather as a pragmatic step for the individual to remain breathing. In step with this, pragmatism remains a steadfast arbiter for many a Satanist's actions, leaving behind impersonal moralisms and restrictive dogmas.

This pragmatism motivated by self-preservation could very well be the unwritten social contract of Satanism. Recognizing man as an animal and accepting that the only inherent rights that any human being has must be taken by wit or force in effect calls for a codifying of a set of guidelines that both celebrates the individual and his animal nature without harming those who do not provoke or deserve his wrath. It is established in Satanism that the line between indulgence and compulsion must be drawn in order to survive (ibid, 81). This is to say that exercising your human potential on Earth is healthy until it produces personal negative consequences, one of which is putting yourself in harm's way when it is unnecessary. Indeed, having to unnecessarily deal with anything appears highly un-Satanic when perusing these examples from "The Eleven Satanic Rules of the Earth:"

> 2. Do not tell your troubles to others unless you are sure they want to hear them.
> 3. When in another's lair, show him respect or else do not go there.
> 8. Do not complain about anything to which you need not subject yourself. (*The Church of Satan*, 85)

When all of this is processed, it appears that both Hobbes and LaVey put no faith in the universal claim of such concepts as good and evil. In fact, in very similar words, LaVey defined the two as thus: "Good is what you like, evil is what you don't like" (*The Devil's Notebook*, 144). When put against Hobbes' longer-winded version of the same idea, a connection is certainly established:

> "Good and evil are names that signify our appetites and aversions, which in different tempers, customs, and doctrines of men are different: and diverse men differ not only in their judgement on the senses of what is pleasant and unpleasant to the taste, smell, hearing, touch, and sight; but also of what is conformable or disagreeable to reason in the actions of common life. Nay, the same man, in diverse times, differs from himself; and one time praiseth, that is, calleth good, what another time he dispraiseth, and calleth evil..." (*Leviathan*, 131)

In all fairness, Hobbes and LaVey would have had their differences. Hobbes professed a belief in an actual God, whereas LaVey did not. LaVey saw the concept of a God, and the religions adhering to this concept, to be useful for a period of ancient history when civilizations were being established, but now largely an outmoded ideology (as a result of education, technology, science, and perhaps even the concentration on reason that many of the Enlightenment figures examined) whose influence is waning fast and being replaced by many pre-Christian ideals, as well as one of many post-Christian arrivals: television. I would also add the Internet as a rapidly-viable component in this new influence.

LaVey would have also had a big problem with Hobbes' assertion that men are generally equal. Aside from physical realities of death and vulnerability to illness, endorsing the notion that intelligence and stupidity, strength and weakness, beauty and ugliness are either inconsequential or on equal footing is both delusional and apologetic. Here, we have an example of Hobbes alluding to some innate equality of man:

> "For as to the strength of body, the weakest has strength enough to kill the strongest, either by secret machination or by confederacy with others that are in the same danger with himself." (*Leviathan*, 105)

What Hobbes is so close to realizing but doesn't quite get is that this supposed "weakest" person was, according to the law of nature, superior in that he was the victor. Many thinkers, writers, and philosophers who have been confronted with a phrase such as "might is right" often shortsightedly assume that it only speaks of physical prowess. The Satanist's view may clarify: the strong dominate the weak, and the clever dominate the strong. Those who have the qualifications to succeed and even excel within their given circumstances and time period simply cannot be given equal consideration with ignorant, lazy and uninspired humans without creating resentment in those who possess great talents and abilities and, at the same time, filling the heads of defective types with delusions of not only unearned adequacy but outstanding achievement as well.

John Locke (1632-1704), another celebrated social contractarian, states that life, liberty and the ownership of property are the chief human rights. But property, in Locke's view, includes more than merely cattle, tools, and homesteads:

> "Though the earth and all inferior creatures be common to all men, yet every man has a 'property' in his own 'person.' This nobody has any right to but himself. The 'labour' of his body and the 'work' of his hands, we may say, are properly his."
> ("Second Essay," Ch.5: 26)

These ideas of property, being body and labor, appear quite analogous to what LaVey expresses in the following statement: "If self preservation is the highest law, the 'self' has its own laws which validate its existence. The first is Stimulation. The second is Identity [both words capitalized by the author]." (*The Devil's Notebook*, 146) Stimulation, in a sense, can be likened to doing that which pleases you or adds meaning to your life. Certainly, laboring for your own favored outcome and taking great pride in your work could count as stimulation. Identity, it would follow, is representative of the body: what it looks like, what you do to it, and what can be done to it by outside forces. If your primary property is your own self, your own body, then it should be of primary concern to preserve it at all costs. Locke would agree to some extent, particularly if the existing government were to intrude on the person in question's immediate safety. In this case, this person would possess the "right" to defend it. Few statements could be more Satanic.

Before we move further, it must be stated that Locke, through reasons of either a personal nature or as a product of his time, supposed the "rights" he speaks of to be granted to mankind by God. Naturally, the Satanist would not subscribe to this view. It is of my opinion that, disregarding the religious references in Locke's work (specifically, those of the assumed Judeo-Christian position), it often stands on its own merits provided you view man in a more carnal sense: man as just another animal, though one with the power of reason.

Locke also believed that if the government became overall tyrannical and ultimately destructive to the people it ostensibly represented, the people have the right -- yea, the duty -- to rebel against and even overthrow that government, an idea that eventually was incorporated by Thomas Jefferson into America's founding documents. Though no fan of total democracy, LaVey understood the importance of casting away any creed, ideal, or doctrine that no longer served a useful purpose, as captured in this synthesis of a Ragnar Redbeard quote:

> "The chief duty of every new age is to upraise new men to determine its liberties, to lead it toward material success -- to rend the rusty padlocks and chains of dead customs that always prevent healthy expansion... As environments change, no human ideal standeth sure." (*The Satanic Bible*, 31)

And, as before with Hobbes, Locke also puts forth that the terms "good" and "evil" are merely associated with personal experience and, by such an assertion, not a universal design:

> "Things then are good or evil, only in reference to pleasure or pain. That we call good, which is apt to cause or increase pleasure, or diminish pain in us; or else to procure or preserve us the possession of any other good or absence of any evil. And, on the contrary, we name that evil which is apt to produce or increase any pain, or diminish any pleasure in us: or else to procure us any evil, or deprive us of any good."
>
> ("Human Understanding," Book 2: Ch. 20)

And, lastly, we come to one of the most influential thinkers of the Enlightenment period: Jean-Jacques Rousseau (1712-1778). Rousseau, like Locke, favored a government with a tentative sovereign power, one revokable if disapproved of -- for legitimate reasons, and not whimsical ones. However, it is Rousseau's curious views concerning God and Christianity that almost express the Satanic view of the God religions in general.

Rousseau, like many latter Enlightenment thinkers, was a Deist, which is to say that although he believed in the existence of a creator deity, this creator, once finished with his production of the universe, left the organisms in it, including man, to their own devices and matters. The Deist god does not intervene in human affairs.

Now, while the Satanist does not believe in the existence of any deities, demons or devils, he may realize the importance of this brave exploration by figures of the past who chose to stray from convention and seek out alternatives. And while Rousseau's morality may have been markedly different from that of Satanism, it may have paved the way for the truly heretical views of Nietzsche, Mencken, and even LaVey.

A case could be made with Rousseau's view of Christianity, which seems far from supportive and mirrors the perspective that Satanism reflects on this religion:

> "Christianity preaches only servitude and dependence. Its spirit is too favorable to tyranny for tyranny not to take advantage of it at all times. True Christians are made to be slaves. They know it and are hardly moved by this." (Rousseau, 101)

One link in the chain of this expressed slavery, according to Rousseau, is money.

Whether by Locke's praising of the pleasure principle (though not because he tries to mash it together with "divine law") or Rousseau's disdain for the monetary system replacing labor done for the sheer enjoyment of creating and innovating, LaVey has often prodded and poked fun at those who confuse the tools of the herd with true happiness. Speaking in appropriately Epicurean terms, LaVey clarifies:

> "[People] are saying 'I must pay dollars for whatever I get in life. You can't be any better than me, so you must pay for what you have in dollars, too.' and then, in the next breath, 'I only want to be appreciated for myself.'...A fit and proper Devil, in order to tempt, must know well the cliched status symbols of common people -- even those with lots of money."
> (*Satan Speaks!*, 133)

All in all, the Enlightenment period may have had some influence on Satanism; in fact, many things did. The Enlightenment's focus on reason, and sometimes even away from the theology of the times, opened a door for many thinkers to come. Nietzsche opened that door a little more in the latter half of the 1800s with his statement, "God is dead," which in turn made it a little less than impossible for the Church of Satan to establish itself in the mid-1960s. In the 21st century, the freedom of expressing anti-Christian and/or anti-authoritarian views is almost taken for granted, and I feel that the individuals mentioned in this essay, intentionally or not, contributed to this expansive environment. How much more it expands will make the journey through this millennium that much more exciting, stimulating and question-provoking.

Works Cited

Barton, Blanche. *The Church of Satan*. New York: Hell's Kitchen. 1990.
Barton, Blanche. *The Secret Life of A Satanist*. New York: Hell's Kitchen. 1990.
Hobbes, Thomas. *Leviathan*. Indianapolis: Bobbs-Merrill. 1958.
LaVey, Anton Szandor. *The Devil's Notebook*. Portland, OR: Feral House. 1992.
LaVey, Anton Szandor. *The Satanic Bible*. New York: Avon. 1969.
LaVey, Anton Szandor. *Satan Speaks!*. Venice, CA: Feral House. 1998.
Locke, John. "Concerning Civil Government, Second Essay." 1690.
Locke, John. "An Essay Concerning Human Understanding." 1690.
Rousseau, Jean-Jacques. *On The Social Contract*. Indianapolis: Hackett. 1987

SATANISM AND RACIALISM: DIVIDING LINES AND COMMON TIES

In the 1990s, the face of Satanism had seen some heretical and herd-deflective manifestations, as any revisionist movement of any significance does. We as ideological archeologists pick and choose principles, ethics, and philosophies from sources considered by the masses as either celebrated or abhorrent -- oftentimes, the latter. Some individuals have pondered Satanism's compatibility with the growing racialist movement (though not for the racial politics). If this seems unlikely, consider this:

> "From every set of principles (be it religious, political, or philosophical), some good can be extracted. Amidst the madness of the Hitlerian concept, one point stands out as a shining example of this -- 'strength through joy!'"
> (- from *The Satanic Bible*, p.82)

One of these philosophical ties that Satanism and many of the racialist movement share is with 19th-century German philosopher Friedrich Nietzsche. Indeed, Nietzsche proved a profound impact on the writings of both Hitler and LaVey; though, two distinct paths were taken by these gentlemen. (Most notable book: Nietzsche's *Der Antichrist*.) Michael Moynihan, in his introduction to his interview with former Rahowa vocalist and then-racialist George Eric Hawthorne writes:

> "... if you care to go beyond media catch-phrases and actually listen to what he has to say, it would undoubtedly fly right over the heads of most redneck racists or Hitlerian hatemongers, as much as it'd rile up the typical liberal humanist."
> (- from *The Black Flame* magazine; Vol. 6, No. 1 & 2, p.40)

Religiously and philosophically, many of those in the racialist movement are blatantly anti-Christian, choosing to align with the Northern European pagan pantheon. (The World Church of the Creator, a racialist organization, is also a fully legal religion, praising the self as a "Creator" and standing as one of the more fervent haters of the Judeo-Christian ideology in the racialist camp.) Runes (ancient divination tools of these Northern Euro-cultures) have shown an archetypal/aesthetic and/or symbolic significance to Odinists, Satanists, neo-Nazis, and racialists; sometimes for similar reasons, sometimes not. The war culture of the ancient Norse people is a shining testament to the glory of superior human traits such as intelligence and performance, akin to the cornerstones of Satanic virtue and certain racialist ideals.

I say certain because, in all fairness, every grouping on Earth will attract different types, and not all measure up to high standards. Below the true Satanists of quality are the wannabes, no-brains, conformists, and music subculture-obsessed that any extreme group will find clinging to its legs. So it is with the racialist movement, though seemingly more tolerant of their leeches:

> "We have National Socialists, and people who hate National Socialism. We have people who honour the American flag, and others who burn it. We have people that believe in the niceness of White Pride, and others that seethe with hatred and call themselves White Supremacists. We have people that are conservative in their opinions, while others are radical and revolutionary. Some of us want a small piece of America, while others want to conquer the world for our kind."
>
> (- from the Resistance Records website)

One of those revolutionaries in the racialist movement is Universal Order head, James Mason. This National Socialist expresses a fondness for the writings of LaVey (and had reprinted, in the Christianity issue of Mason's former newsletter *SIEGE*, a section of "The Book of Satan" from LaVey's *The Satanic Bible*) though not a fan of encouraging law-abiding behavior:

> "Well, I think Anton LaVey advocates good citizenship -- using your intelligence and not laboring under any superstitions -- but

> at the very bottom of it, be a good citizen. And I don't advocate being a good citizen -- I advocate subverting society... there's a lot of common ground [between groups]. You maintain a certain kind of standard that's only going to attract a certain kind of person. With him, it's Satanism. With us, it's with the swastika."
>
> (- from *OHM Clock* magazine; Issue 3, p.9)

So, again, it's a matter of taking what you agree with and discarding that which is against your individual nature. Or against nature in general, for that matter. Much is why both racialists and Satanists typically take an anti-Christian stance: because the Christian religion (and most of the other "major" religions) is truly anti-nature. (This, again, figures into Nietzschean philosophy, as well as the writings of Ragnar Redbeard. Conversely, this excludes the mass of Ku Klux Klan members, many of whom subscribe to the Christian Identity movement: a group that believes that the White Race is the chosen people of their god, and that the Jews are descended from "Satan." The largest racialist group to personify this mindset is Aryan Nations.) Both (especially Satanists) despise the allowances given to people who invariably display parasitic behavior upon society. Intelligence and performance are the standard and immutable rule in Satanism, whereas race criteria come into play (sometimes, in addition to our checklist items) with racialists. Consider the following for either philosophy:

> "...we have an obligation to the Nature of which we are a part to participate as effectively as we can in its eternal quest for higher levels of development, higher forms of life. This obligation has been recognized and expressed by our poets and philosophers throughout our history... Nietzsche told us that our first responsibility is to help prepare the world for the coming of a higher type of man. George Bernard Shaw wrote that we are obliged to serve the Life Force in its striving to know itself more fully (i.e.: to achieve higher levels of consciousness)."
>
> (- from the National Alliance website)

Particularly for the aforementioned group, the hierarchy racialists ascribe to this human worth is (perhaps, surprisingly) not just measured from race to race, with the White Man on top. Concerning whites, this uncredited racialist author agrees:

> "They [whites] come in many forms. From the overeducated, liberal media prostitutes that grovel before their Ashkenazi masters with offerings of anti-White propaganda; to the soulless materialist men and women... right down to the semi-retarded rural and urban dwelling dirt, there are undoubtedly legions of clamoring fools and character-deficient low-lifes that masquerade as White due to their pale pigmentation... we White Racialists only respect White people that deserve respect, and hold in low-esteem Whites who deserve our contempt. If anything, our recognition of the abundant supply of White losers only reinforces our belief that all men are not created equal."
> (- from the Resistance Records website)

Spread to a more inclusive plane, those are truly beautiful, misanthropic words any Satanist could appreciate. Not entirely amazing, this is not the media picture painted side-by-side with the dominant PC-rhetoric in current rotation, from the corporate cable news channels to the "hippest" zines (both illusively priding themselves on "objective" reporting).

And it's this insecurity of the herd and its reflective media that cloud the perception of any being who strives for higher ground. Satanists and racialists are vastly and vehemently shunned by certain parts of society (though, Satanists may get substantially less of this backlash, depending on situation, location, and people). One could say that we are even feared -- and for good reason -- though not for many of the propagated "horrors." Herein lies a difference between many racialist groups and us: Racialists, understandably so, do not want to be the minority (either racially or ideologically); Satanists, knowing that we are a minority, are quite happy (and often quite giddy) to be such and, in many cases, encourage the human dross to steer clear of us. For some Satanists, it becomes unproductive to promote otherwise.

To facilitate the elements of attempted (and defensively projected) fear and ostracism toward us (the collective us, mind you), the mainstream media enlist their core troops from what seems to be some centralized propaganda department and direct them to those they can cash in on the quickest: Satanism and racialism are two of the more popular; the more convoluted the definition, the bigger the paycheck.

(Just ask Jerry Springer.) Both of us, as if by some incredibly unoriginal group of ad execs, are portrayed as "gang members" (oh, you haven't read the Christian-aimed-at-law-enforcement propagandist pap trying desperately to peg Satanists as "gang-related?" It's out there, believe me), "hate criminals," and generally of a mindless and uncontrollably violent nature. Resistance Records writes in adequate defense to these claims:

> "Television is saturated with violence, and our young people spend endless days playing video games like Mortal Kombat... [in addition,] Hard Metal, Gangsta Rap, 'anti-racist' hardcore like Rage Against The Machine, and several other genres of music, are laden with violent images and concepts... but they are afforded artistic license to speak their minds and rise up the *Billboard* charts with virtually no opposition... to those that claim that White Racialists represent an image that is any more violent than the rest of this demented society, look them straight in the eye and declare them a hypocrite."
>
> (-from the Resistance Records website)

Of course, these terms used -- hate crimes, in particular -- are thoroughly subjective. Hate is fine in the United States... as long as its forms fall neatly into the anal-retentive pegholes of social acceptability and political correctness. (And there are comparative levels on which the herd are allowed to judge religions. For example: Christianity is somewhat okay to pick on; and perhaps moreso with the passing years. However, Judaism is verbotten. Can't scrutinize that religion; after all, "they" had a holocaust, don't you know. Let it be known that this Satanist is fully unrepentant in his understanding that these religions, in a core sense, are two sides of the same coin.) "Smash the racists' right to have websites" is okay. "Smash affirmative action" is not okay. If I read the meter correctly, any unorthodox racial viewpoint publicly expressed (especially in our obsessively sensitive American culture) elicits a more emphatic condemnation than murder. Severe, but you get the idea. Free speech is for the fresh-breathed. Democracy is for the pretty people.

And neither of us is, in the largely social sense, pretty. We take that unto ourselves to some degree and, in the Satanist's case, use it to our best advantage, knowing full well an unswerving human truth: Society without its devils (even its White devils) is an unchallenged society: weak, non-analytical, complacent and delusional; and I mean sizably moreso than it already is. Just as Satan, the accuser, will always (yet, sometimes covertly) swing the social pendulum in the other direction every once in awhile in the name of balance, so will racialism ferret out race issues that may be worth looking at, regardless of those who (in cowardice) would rather not discuss anything related to such "sensitive" topics (e.g.: race, gender, class, etc.) for fear of offending someone, presumedly anyone. In this world of say-nothings and safe smiles, I'd rather offend than pretend, at my discretion; the very fire behind both Satan and swastika.

IF VOTING CHANGED ANYTHING... I'D STILL LAUGH!

As many know, I am no fan of democracy. In most cases, it is the political representative for Judeo-Christian values in the United States (and, now abroad with the U.S. Government's sweep to democratize the world), regardless of how many armchair "freethinkers" wish to paint it in pretty secular colors. Luckily, democratic influence in American politics is limited, and that the originally intended Republic is still, more or less, in place. [Insert "The Imperial March" from the *Star Wars* soundtrack here.] And, although I don't always agree with all that constitutes a Republic -- and, in fact, do not take either of the cookie-cutter positions of republican or democrat, left or right, good or evil, black or white, or any other God-religion inspired duality -- it's a far better system than the frightening scenario of actual rule "by the people." Have you taken a good look at "the people" lately? Not exactly a nation of those fit to rule, let alone those able to think for themselves. Rather, they should stick to what they know best: reality TV, pop culture, baseball scores, club hopping, and unquestioningly believing the media.

Likewise, I do not vote. Why? Well...

I don't kid myself into believing that politicians have my best interests in mind, or that putting "faith" in one unfamiliar human being (read: God substitute) is a noble gesture, or that elected candidates follow through with election promises (or even can), or that the voting system is anywhere near accurate or representative (of me? of them? who knows until it's too late?), and I certainly have enough sense to avoid the almost religious fervor of voter drives, replete with glassy-eyed college kids waving their registration forms like so many bibles, preaching their sidewalk sermons on the virtues of voting, democracy, the system, brotherhood, peace and love, etc. In the age of the God religions losing significant influence on secular society, while at the same time our culture is filled with those who need to believe in something, anything, it appears that the voting crusaders want a piece of the belief pie left behind (often starting with the ludicrous fantasy of "world peace"). I believe Redbeard referred to similar occurrences as "a beautiful hoodwink." Throw in Machiavelli, and you get the point.

And that's great, so long as it doesn't intrude upon my life. Pragmatically speaking, I like the fact that the masses vote, abuse drugs, believe in Jesus, follow sports, and worship a flag. They are tools of social engineering that keep the many-too-many sedate, pacified, and out of many people's hair (chiefly, my own). Sure, the extremists exist, but the majority of believers (either religious or secular) serve a useful and less intrusive purpose as consumers and laborers, as their nature dictates. So, don't assume that I am against (other people's) participation in the voting process. It's a placebo for them, and a spectacle to me.

The only rare exception I would make concerning voting would be with local ballot initiatives (a significantly different animal), but then it would have to be something I could get behind, possess tangible proof of efficacy, and that such change would affect me, and that may or may not ever come. In the meantime, I'm not exactly holding my breath.

Everybody's Out To Get Me!
Your Guide To Social Scapegoats

Scapegoatting has become a veritable lifestyle for so many human groupings. From such socially-approved side-shifting, it's evident that the difference between citizen and sucker (for the majority, anyway) is all a matter of timing, with the status quo being the stopwatch. The common man, in order to maintain a semblance of competence and integrity, has to blame someone -- otherwise he'd have to face the hard fact of any organism's life: that the individual isn't all-powerful and that some parts of life are either unexplainable or not entirely controllable. No point in whining about it once that truth is realized. In fact, once you can accept this reality, most of life's supposed "enemies" are ferreted out and exposed for the paper tigers that they've always been. Some parts of life are irrelevant, or at least have so little to do with the citizenry that to gnaw and chew on them as if they were, collectively, some pseudo-intellectual rubber bone makes the herd look even more like the nominal people that most of them potentially are. Questions often unasked: Is this really worth worrying about? Does this really have anything to do with me or am I just caught up in the prepackaged soap opera like everyone else? The tragic comedy of it all: Most of them will never get it and would most likely give up their iPods or mocha latte addictions before they'd admit to such a rude awakening. Like sands through the hour-glass...

So are the numerous catch-phrases which accompany these aggregate mindsets. You know them well because you hear them perpetuated in common speech, in well-insulated music and social cliques and, of course, such use of language can make an insecure, weak, and/or stupid person seem "discerning", "culturally-aware", "insightful" or just plain "cool." In theory, they're better off than the dupes they mock, those who consume the obvious soma without reservation and without regard. In practice, they're as separated from each other as David Berkowitz is from mental illness.

With such a comparison model, little indeed disassociates the armchair revolutionist from the street-cruising, beer-swilling, small-town farm teen, save the variance in self-glorification. So, ladies and gentlemen, HERE ARE THE TOKEN COMBATANTS...

THE GOVERNMENT

"History proves that man is a beast of prey. The beast of prey conquers countries, founds great realms by subjugation of other subjugators, forms states and organizes civilizations in order to enjoy his booty in peace... Attack and defense, suffering and struggle, victory and defeat, domination and servitude, all sealed with blood; this is the entire history of the human race." - Richard Wagner

Some people -- realistically, a slim minority of them -- probably have legitimate gripes with the Federal Government of the United States. Bad things do indeed happen to good people, though not as often as the current victim culture likes to purport. So, putting away those scant few instances of actual governmental injustice, let's look at the rest of The People.

Perhaps the first thing lost is the global perspective. Americans (and only by residence would I consider myself to be one... not because of the government, but because of "those people") have the keys to the golden whorehouse, yet are the first to bitch when their toilet paper isn't scented or embossed with pretty flowers. Admit it! We love being in the most powerful country in the world. And apparently, other people do, too, as evidenced by our soaring immigration rates. Yet through some collective misfire of the brain, some just can't face the reality that it takes some serious iron-fistedness to become and remain a dominant nation.

Even from the time of this republic's emergence, blood was unavoidably spilled. And, one of the most precious and delicate flowers purportedly raped and crushed underfoot by our founding fathers was our dealing with the American Indians during the European settlement.

Why is it that transplants from Siberia (as if they were "natives" to this land, either) are given such politically-correct dispensation when most Indian tribes came from a war culture as well? Would you like to know why? Because "we" had bigger weapons. It's that simple. The winners never bellyache and the losers never throw a party. Welcome to the crux of civilization. Is this at all new to you? And why?

Virtually every civilization on Earth was built upon the backs of the previous tenants. But why are Siberian-Americans exempt from having blood on their hands and held up as special? What makes their lives worth any more than any other tribe, clan, or people? Because their so-called plight is relatively recent? When it's the Holy Crusades, it's called history, but when it's the Pilgrims or, even more recently, the Nazis, it's an atrocity. It's not the numbers that frighten the sheep, it's the proximity of time. It bugs them because the bodies aren't quite cold enough for them. And, they're too scared to disagree with the dominant social climate. I mean, what would their coffeehouse pals say?

I'm well educated to the reality that war -- or even the threat of war -- is often the chief way to establish civilizations and the most effective way to keep them. Some people are squeamish about that. Can't be helped. Aging hippies and misguided college kids alike can throw all of the peace-and-pot rallies they want. They can protest, postulate, and clutch their new-age crystals (crucifixes?) until the harmonic convergence comes home. None of this is going to turn folks like Osama bin Laden or Kim Jong-Il into good little boys. Not even if we give them free internet access.

Sure, our current government has problems. Depending on who you are, you'll probably have a different complaint list than the next bunch of people, all scrambling up to the podium to see who can shout the loudest or make the biggest spectacle of themselves, continuing to disagree with each other, assuming one thing's good for everyone and trying to push dissenters underthumb. Gee, that sounds like a *government*!

THE POLICE

"It's very simple: More cops, fewer problems. Take away the cops, lose everything. You'd all be buzzard meat without police. Erase the thin blue line, and your brains will be soapsuds smeared all over the streets. Because the 'cream' which will rise to power under pure an-

archy will behave exactly like the cops, only they won't be muzzled by law. If you think police brutality is bad, wait until mob brutality replaces it." - Jim Goad

A favored token enemy of punkers and Rodney King worshipers, as well as the very *real* enemy of unadmitted (and not so subtle) lawbreakers of all colors and smells. Police have the most thankless job on the planet, and the Great Unwashed only insist on reminding them of it with their ingrate attitudes, generalizations, and saliva. They're pissed on, shot at, griped to and generally treated miserably; all because people are generally sneaky and shifty little vermin who want to get away with doing everything, but don't want anything done to them. I, for one, love cops! They push that hypocritical parasite-politic in the faces of scumbags like only a caring and firm father would. For those about to patrol, I salute you.

Every time I hear "fuck the cops" from someone, I hope 911 gives them a busy signal. Like ungrateful children, they bitch and moan about the few bad eggs that they assume to be the whole bunch, calling for the death of all of them without giving a thought about what they'd do without them. Thin blue line? They're the Hoover Dam at this point, if you compare the possibility of not having them to the reality of the reverse. Is anyone really ready to gamble with an unpoliced tribe of humans acting civil and forming "collectives" on the heads of your kids, your lovers, your spouses and friends?

The only people who want the cops out of the way are usually the ones who have such self-loathing that they see no reason to not bring on the anarchy. Why is it so amazing that certain individuals can hang so securely to the thread that keeps them alive when nature has already read their death sentences? Most of these people would be better off dead, and practically beg for it, either done by someone else's hands (for being a social parasite) or their own (out of lack of self-respect, self-confidence, and most of the other negative self-_____s). Kill a cop? Kill yourself, you useless piece of dung. Leave life to us who want it, and to the cops for keeping it all cleaned up around us.

THE WHITE MAN

"I'm sorry/ For something I didn't do/ Lynched somebody/ But I don't know who/ You blame me for slavery/ A hundred years before I was born/ Guilty of being white." - Minor Threat

This social scapegoat is a favorite of certain members of the female gender and various ethnicities (particularly, those of African or Hispanic descent) in love with being active participants in the current victim culture. These aren't exactly the great thinkers of our time, but, oh, how they spend their lives in a sour grapes obsession that, more times than not, doesn't involve them or doesn't exist. But some folks do like to get good and worked up. And, why not? It lessens the blow of economic retardation, of little to no education, and of the other favorite Darwinian tests of drugs, crime, and poverty. (And, most importantly, *it's at someone else's expense*.) All of these, of course, can be blamed on a particular racial and gender-specific grouping. That's right! White men! I should know. I'm white, and I'm male... and I'm heterosexual! Am I the big, bad, world-dominating oppressor of the masses or what?!

The inconvenient reality is that I'm not oppressing anyone. But, I can see how the provision of some testosterone conspiracy becomes the soft and cuddly story that whiners can curl up with when the hard knocks of life come creeping outside the windows. Because of the past (a past neither you nor I were a part of), *I'm* to blame when someone doesn't take school seriously enough to get good grades, or why someone has seven kids and on welfare by the time they're 21, or why they're strung out on drugs, etc. Apparently, I also possess some sort of mind control.

Those who blame another race for their own shortcomings should consider themselves lucky that nature has nothing to say about their delusions. Thinking that way in a less civilized setting would mean death, and their bodies would serve their only inherent purposes: food and fertilizer. If this seems unpleasant, then maybe take a cue from reality. Intelligence. Performance. *Those* are the healthy choices. Go with them.

THE FASHION INDUSTRY/ THE BEAUTIFUL PEOPLE

"Fat people who bash thin people and whine about society's attitude about fat are simply betraying, in a painfully obvious and embarrassing manner, their envy and resentment of those who by nature

or self-discipline have healthier and more attractive bodies and are reaping the rewards which come with this." - J. Deboo

Nothing helps the herd feel better about their inadequacies than lambasting those who have their missing attributes. Instead of facing the hard, cold fact that they're unbecoming or obese, these protesters against public attractiveness rail against the very media that reflects social beauty; primarily, the fashion industry. Talk about scapegoat soufflé!

In this war of Ugg versus Ahh, a plague of feminist sob sisters charge up the hill, burning effigies of Paris Hilton (it *is* all her fault, you know), rallying to the cause that femininity has been ill-represented in society, and that we should all realize that the true definition is angry, misandrist (i.e.: someone who hates men) lesbians (and even *ersatz* lesbians) with macho haircuts on their heads and penis envy in their minds. That's right, folks. We're all deluded. They *must* be right. They've got non-profit organizations, after all.

Forget the glamor mags, the billboard images, and the beer commercials! Here's the *real* problem: People are trying to screw outside of their looks group. Yes, you read that correctly. Everyone, according largely to physical attributes (though, others play a near-existent secondary role), has a limited spectrum of possible sexual partners falling into roughly the same range. Dumbo doesn't get lucky with Snow White, and there's no way that the ugly stepsisters could ever score a threesome with Prince Charming. In Satanism, we refer to this as one example of having a keen awareness of the Balance Factor. Or, for the uninitiated: know your limitations or rely on the ambivalent horniness of damaged people and veteran drunks.

As for the multitudinous busybodies of the world, here's some food for thought: Those who stick their noses in other people's affairs never have any affairs to speak of. That's because they're probably UGLY!

THE "AVERAGE JOES"

"After an inferior man has been taught a doctrine of superiority he will remain as inferior as he was before his lesson. He will merely assume himself to be superior, and attempt to employ his recently-learned tactics against his own kind, whom he will then consider his inferiors. With each inferior man enjoying what he considers his unique role, the entire bunch will be reduced to a pack of strutting, foppish, self-centered monkeys gamboling about on an island of ignorance. There they will play their games under the supervision of their keeper, who was and will always be a superior man."

- Anton Szandor LaVey

Yes. It's the great, inflated and equally premeditated enemy of all self-important "countercultures:" the "Average Joes." In practice: a shoddily crafted and patently transparent bigotry often practiced by those who cloak themselves with a fashion/ideological façade in order to distract the closest sub-herds away from just how stupid, piss-boring, ugly, obnoxious and/or meaningless the accusers really are. It really gets to some folks that they are, under close inspection, as normal as the people they point fingers at, and this inextricable link certainly doesn't get the wannabe-different the attention it so blatantly craves (and isn't that what it's all about?). So, someone has to take the fall for this. Why not the normals?

Since I've seen what we shall call the "Anti-average" in action through numerous "scenes" and towns spanning many states in our great nation, let me give you the typical prognosis:

I've always found these desperate souls in search of gratuitous abnormality rather bad actors and actresses (and, ironic or not, they often have this burning desire for the career of acting. If not, then something involving art, with psychology running a close third), but perhaps that's a deeper point. Sometimes the script is purposely fubbed, as this person clearly wishes to be rescued of some psychosis, emotional instability or general insecurity and self-confidence problem. (Many of the previous categories in this essay are rife with such motives.) Maybe, they just want us all to be impressed with how "vulnerable" they are. Quite honestly, how can anyone (ostensibly or nay) bother themselves with whether or not other people are "normal" unless they aren't all that secure with themselves to begin with? The reason they bother is due to the fact that they live such monotonous and ineffectual lives, they must vicariously feed upon someone else's life. In this respect, the Anti-average lives his/her self-loathing and depression by projecting it upon the "Average Joes," thereby achieving some purgation and avoiding the reality of just how sad and wretched their own lives really are. But, alas. Time for the curtain call.

The Anti-average often enough attaches itself to one or more suitable hosts, for both a social life and to seem "not ordinary." Generally, the choice of host(s) is made selectively, or as selective as any mentally-deficient mind can get; preferably, hosts of an intellectual or "socially-hostile" nature. On the rare chance, it could be someone who is actually of the true anti-social bent but, often enough, those types recognize a parasite for what it is and move on. No, the Anti-average, compromisingly, tends to gravitate to the bargain basement variety of social inepts, glorified losers, and people who are generally better (even slightly better) than they are. This fragile little bonding will often facilitate numerous social gatherings, from which the Anti-average can appropriate bits and pieces of heretical and/or controversial philosophy, and fling them aimlessly with all of the zeal of a toddler who's recently discovered his/her genitals and just won't leave them alone. Needless to say, if the Anti-average can actually not siphon off of other people's conversation and come up with an independent thought, it will be grossly embarrassing, shortsighted, painfully derivative and even immature on the occasion. And, Hell forbid, if they really *do* have a psychosis, it's typically a bland and flavorless one. Even in mental illness, these people are humdrum. If there was an award for this accomplishment, they'd debate whether to take it and seem "cool" or refuse it and save face. Oh, the humanity!

There are numerous other possible categories -- probable candidates include The Rich, The Music Industry, The Opposite Sex (or The Same Sex, depending), The Religious Right, or any other well-timed thorn in the sides of the many, be it contrived or incidental. And while the low-grade drama of rampant attention-getting unfolds, the Satanist can sit back and removedly enjoy the amusement of it all, knowing he or she will never be an easy mark for such social shenanigans.

BANGIN' IN LITTLETON

Television sets around the nation were aglow and tuned into *the* main event on the evening of April 20th, 1999. The sheep clutched each other in horror as the tacitly "acceptable" killing in Kosovo was pre-empted for the terrifying closer-to-home drama of two disgruntled teenagers who decided to go postal (or is that go pupil?) on 12 classmates and a teacher to express their deep-seated resentment and, judging from the more-wounded-than-dead ratio, their bad aim. Just visualize *Revenge of The Nerds* with better fashion sense and access to really big guns. Or, in light of the killers blowing their own brains out as a grand finale, maybe it's *Heathers* with a bigger body count? They even purportedly chose the birth anniversary of the Third Reich's main man to further fuel the public outrage. What's more, they even listened to... gasp!... Marilyn Manson, Rammstein, and KMFDM. What's a concerned parent to do?

Apparently, the brainless but ever-popular answer to that last question is to listen to the out-of-touch media's ludicrous suggestions that we blame guns, music, video games and even the entire black trenchcoat industry. I tell you, it's a damn bleating hysteria out there. And they say that there's a conspirator still on the loose. Careful! Look under your beds tonight before going to sleep! It's a heartless and out of control generation -- just ask the newspeople.

As the story unfolded, many Satanists were merely waiting for the mindless inevitability: the media's throwing down of the Satan card. Once it was discovered that the deceased gunmen listened to "gothic" music (i.e.: the aforementioned bands who are, by and large, *not* considered to be within the gothic genre by that grouping's longest held members -- not that our media would ever get something wrong, mind you) and that they may or may not have had an interest in Hitler and Nazi

Germany, some link, even the weakest, oblique, and/or most erroneous links to us, had to be proclaimed. Parents and journalists unite in a frenzy of blameshifting and sensationalism, ignoring that pesky evidence to the contrary.

That annoying little fact that inconveniently exists is that the gunmen were the furthest thing from being Satanists. *The Satanic Bible* goes into plenty of reasons why they wouldn't be welcomed on the Left Hand Path (stupidity, being the biggest one), so you can do the research if you need to. No, I'd like to discuss why, on some level, I'm not choked up about all of this bloodshed.

First off, the Littleton mass murder has spawned more than its share of self-righteous (key word there) indignation from pulpit-pounding preachers, slimy politicians (and those who just want to be them), and two-dimensionally thinking parents, all who have taken the spotlights thrust upon them to point fingers at everyone and never dare examine their own role in all of this. While witnessing this fiasco, I'm reminded that any chance to expose the general ignorance, stupidity and blind conformist values of our fellow citizens is fine with me, and, dare I say it, vastly entertaining. It's like *The Jerry Springer Show*: the real freaks are the myopic, spoonfed audience members.

Let's start with the preachers or, more importantly, the religion behind them: Christianity. Littleton, Colorado is a glaring example of a Christian yuppified, planned community-type caricature of all of those less-than-tolerant '60s sitcom locations. I've even lived in about a half-dozen of those constricting little Rocky Mountain towns, and many of them have this startling parallel (and it's no small coincidence that Focus On The Family and Bob Larson Ministries both claim Northern Colorado as their home territory -- it's the last loop in the Bible Belt, if you ask me). I mean, have you seen so many bake sale moms and soccer dads, apparently time-frozen, in any one place in your lives? Taken as a whole, these ingredients are a recipe for outcast-goes-loopy. When you force anti-human Christian values and impossible to attain moralisms upon kids whose marked intelligence repels them from such a servile and unconditionally accepted mindset, don't be surprised if he/she lashes back in resentment. Consider the murders in Littleton to be that frustration exponentiated and, to some degree, a product of what happens when you push Jesus on people who aren't stupid or needy enough to swallow it.

Next come the politicians. These government-paid actors know that to get (and stay) elected, they must ride the crest of a bogeyman scare, no matter how contrived. Once, the enemy of the State we all had to fear was those scurvy Communists, then the Russians in general, then nuclear war, pit bulls, "devil worshipers," terrorism, drugs, militias, and now we can look forward to the latest propped-up paper tiger we'll all be told to run in mortal terror from: our own outcast teenagers! So, the hucksters will get on their red, white and blue soapboxes and wax nauseous over how it's all the fault of the guns, that Duke Nukem leads to butchering your entire high school, and that, in order for criminals to no longer get their illegal guns, we must yank guns away from legal owners. This is comparable to proposing that the foolproof panacea to drunk driving is to ban alcohol and automobiles. Think it couldn't possibly get any more asinine?

Let's chat a few about the parents (and the bulk of the more visible citizenry) of Littleton, as well as their automaton Stepford children, who, by the way, seemed suspiciously beaming when those cameras were initially aimed at their apple-cheeked little faces.

Littleton parents and kids alike, when interviewed, were, along with other expressions of naiveté, using terms that were vastly out of touch with the outside world, let alone the '90s. (One kid said that the "goth" gunmen listened to "acid rock," a term that went out with '70s arena bands.) Many of them said they didn't understand why the shootings happens. I thought, "that's exactly *why* they happened."

It doesn't seemed too far fetched that after all of the overplayed funeral eulogies of adolescent cherubs praising Jesus to an obsessive-compulsive degree, this sleepy little hamlet was in fact a viper's nest of collectivized Christians who didn't like or simply couldn't understand people who felt, thought, and/or dressed differently than themselves. In this regard, the well-intended folks of Littleton has unintentionally brought this whole mess upon their own heads, and there is no number of recitations of the Lord's Prayer that'll change that.

Simply stated, the lesson of Littleton isn't about the tragedy of children being killed (or the assumption that hides behind that, such as the death of an adult being somehow "less" tragic than that of a teenager), or about the supposed accessibility of guns, or even about a stricter "moral" code. It's far more immediate and realistic than all of that hoopla: be careful who you systematically terrorize, pick on or put down, because they might just come back to put a bullet in your head. It would be ideal if the student body of Columbine High School went home that April evening with such a rude awakening burned into their minds, but that's being optimistic and unreasonably expecting the mass of teen sheep to be able to process anything without the impersonal ethics of their parents straining every bit of information they gather.

Don't get me wrong here. I'm not saying that slaughtering people is the way to solve your every problem. And neither am I saying that ending up a suicide statistic is a noble thing; in fact, it's a damn meaningless gesture that will be easily forgotten when the next social scare comes down the electronic pike. The gunmen could have easily stuck it out until they graduated and then left Jesusville. They could have defended themselves in non-lethal ways by learning proper self-defense, instead of ending up as their two last victims. Or, they could have taken the time to realize (or asked someone a tad older than themselves) that most of the so-called popular kids end up the most directionless losers after their social life-support machine gives out. For many, it's their self-perpetuating curse. But just think. Eric and Dylan, instead of being two dead kids, could have been customers of mine. Now, I feel bad for them!

But, the logical point to address here is that, no matter how much the herd strives for it, we do not live in a completely child safety-guarded society. Frustrated people with grudges will explode, often in messy and socially inappropriate ways, and there is nothing you can do about it except for staying on their good side, being able enough to duck in time, or simply having the good fortune of not being around when the lead starts spraying. No abundance of "education" is going to make being crammed into an insulting and alien peghole seem hunky dory to some folks. Dress codes won't help, either.

Perhaps if "being different" wasn't such a cultural crime in many communities, the frustration and anger behind acts such as these might not have even developed. Robert Kennedy once said that "every society gets the kind of criminal it deserves." And while I wouldn't whitewash the very serious complicity of these two young men, I would also point out that the first step towards such vengeful mass murder often begins with being treated poorly in the younger years.

Suffer the little children, as one failed prophet said.

EVERYTHING I LEARNED TO HATE ABOUT PEOPLE, I LEARNED IN KINDERGARTEN

It's strange what folks remember regarding their childhoods: Some remember their first kiss, or the first time they rode their bicycle without Mom or Dad holding onto the back of the seat, or even some tragic accident or event that seems so silly now. Me? I remember kindergarten... with vivid recall.

It's been said before that we've learned most of the important stuff for life in kindergarten. I agree. It is also theorized that a human's psychological profile is complete by age five, the common age for children attending kindergarten. I'll buy some of that. After all, I learned quite a bit. But, not exactly the skills and mechanisms they wanted of me. Through process of elimination, or maybe just having half a brain, I was the ideological AWOL of the class. As if that should be a challenge.

Kindergarten isn't so much about learning as it is about brainwashing via drone repetition, followed by years of a society scratching their heads, wondering why its citizens are such puppets and automatons. It's also where a budding, young misanthrope learns his own nature, that first realization that these diminutive creatures whose only relation to you is immediate space, age, and involuntary fashion are intellectually paralleled to the family dog, and that you'll get to share airspace with them for the next twelve years. If dogs are what I was surrounded by for those eight hours a day, then kindergarten was certainly the Obedience Training School. Consider these examples culled from my own experience as testimony:

Hokey-Pokey: Everyone remembers this little "conformity as fun" game. The entire class gets in either a regimented circle or some sort of orderly geometric configuration while singing this ridiculous song, demanding you take some assigned part of your body, put in into the circle, take it out, put it back in, and "shake it all about." What this game is to us more intellectually-prepared five-year-olds is a clear method of flagging the Darwinian rejects. You *don't* remember them? They were the ones who were not only participating, but they were actually *excited* about doing this retarded motor-skills/mind-suck dance, with an eye on his/her peers and teacher for some sort of emotional group hug. Needless to say, I spent Hokey-Pokey time in the corner out of total refusal to participate. I didn't have the vocabulary then that I do now, but I knew what was going on: Hokey-Pokey was nothing more than a cheap excuse to learn conformity, and be forced to interact with common children who would grow up to be even more common adults.

Nap-Time: This, undoubtedly, kept most of the rug-rats shut for a good 30 minutes or so. I simply *loved* nap time. After so many hours of being harassed by bored little post-tykes who wanted me to "play" with them, to teachers trying to force such a directive until the words become some cacophonous blur of white noise, that amount of time on that slightly-uncomfortable green cot was utter bliss. No noise, no frenetic activity, no more pre-grade school lesson drills, just lots of time for me to think up all that creative stuff that growing up tends to molest us of and would just be punished for in first grade, anyway.

Pledge of Allegiance: This may not be valid today in some kindergartens, but when I was five (1973-1974), we all got to be drilled in this propaganda piece every morning -- that time of the day when you're too tired to put up a fight. "You got to get them while they're young," cry all of the religionists, and this is about as close as the government gets to a Hail Mary.

As could be imagined, I simply couldn't swallow the whole "God" concept, which pops up towards the end of that pledge. The notion of gods was okay as a good story, but at five (as now), the Christian god was considerably boring, trapped in a book that was even more lackluster. But, I knew the effect of the word on my pint-sized classmates and teacher. One class, after our holy communion of Kool-aid and cookie, the teacher (or glorified babysitter) asked what we wanted to be when we grew up (as if most of the kids had *any* solid clue), I announced that I wanted to be God! I said it with an almost menacing tone but the teacher, braindead and assuming I meant the popular interpretation, gushed over me and asked me what wonderful and loving things I would do as God. I told her I would wreak havoc, cause earthquakes, floods, disease, and basically wipe out most of the population, all because it looked like a hell of a lot of fun. Basically, a little boy's answer. (Imagine my receptivity to video games, circa 1979.) With that, I earned myself some well-wanted alienation from most of the class.

To add insult to inanity, there were other mindless exercises of equally unimportant proportion around the corner; outside play time seemed to invite them torrentially. One that still baffles me to this very day involved this scaled-down replica of a log cabin we had in the play area outside. Through some misfire of the brain, the teacher thought this faux-domicile to be the perfect focus-point for children and, thus, developed a completely absurd activity to encompass it. At the break, the teacher would allow a small number of children (usually 3-6) a bucket of water and one standard-sized paint-brush each: the kind used for painting fences and larger structures. In turn, these midget Einsteins would paint the outside of the cabin laboriously... with water. In effect, the water made the wood appear to be about four shades darker (for a time, depending on weather) than previously, hence, the illusion of productivity and yet another test to sort out the mentally-competent from those who are obscenely fascinated with bright, shiny objects and gurgle on the drop of a dime at the sight of an active television screen.

Perhaps, a more long-term example is called for. One stalwart method of early social indoctrination whose susceptibility belongs to the young and credulous, or is a direct introductory guidance to useless mechanisms in general is that of encouraging substance-challenged relationships. To be more specific, we begin to learn to like people (or are convinced that we feel that we like people) for no valid reasons. This is probably one of the earliest times when we are smacked on the wrists for being discerning or at least particular about who we'd like to have around us, in effect, cheapening the term "friendship." (Later, and probably as an extension of this devaluation, the herd nurse this virus and deceive themselves far too willingly by convoluting love with everything but.)

Of course, who can forget the most pervasive socializing contraption in existence: television. There have been so many studies on the effects of television on children, enough to show that TV kids need to be constantly entertained and have trouble playing solitarily. Now, I liked cartoons as much as the next rug-rat, and did a fair share of television viewing myself, so there must be an element missing; something that doesn't connect me to them. Perhaps, I'm answering my own question; maybe it's a matter *of* connectivity. Television, to me, was trite amusement; to others, someone else's "memories" to live and discuss with other addicts. (I've heard enough junkies tell me that other junkies are the only relatable folks. Give that a thought.) But, even as small children, so many humans really need those stories (just like collecting band stories, sports stories, etc.), mostly because it patches into our desire to be storytellers yet replaces legitimate stories with pre-fab ones. Not only are most humans forming meaningless relationships, but telling meaningless stories as well. This may not be directly related to kindergarten curricula, but here's the first grouping you see it in. And, as if the teachers are paid enough to care or know what to do, seeing as they were television kids, too. In the words of Mr. Gump: Stupid is as stupid does.

So, thanks for the lessons. Realistically, I could have spent the day at the zoo and learned the same sermon. With the exception that non-human animals have an excuse, and they're critical of their surroundings enough to not always be agreeable with them. It's their *awareness* that thrives when most of the human sheep simply lose or suppress theirs. The only way to survive kindergarten and the nauseating years of public school to follow is that keeping of awareness. If you got to hang onto that, you're either a Satanist, or just plain lucky.

The Black Suit In Both Theory and Application

Unlike the social provocation that can predictably come with wearing darkly-hued music subcultural uniforms, the iconography of the black suit is in a class all by itself. The combination of that dread color (black) and the status of an accepted cultural emblem (the suit) carries with it a great power. More importantly, it is a power often not recognized by those upon whom it effectively influences. Donned by the herd-savvy Satanist, it becomes a prime weapon in the arsenal of Lesser Magic, a push/pull dynamic that can truly "confound and confuse" while, at the same time, allowing the Satanist to respectively implant the right impressions into the right people and benefit from each individual summation regardless of third-party opinion.

To gain even a working sense of this dynamic is to recognize that the black suit has different meanings or purposes for different Satanists. With many, it is a personal and not necessarily vocalized pride in themselves as iconoclasts, as individuals, and/or their natural alignment with the Satanic archetype -- an archetype defined by us and not others. It can be a statement of human potential, or knowledge and utilization of the means by which our world operates, or a separation from those who choose to adorn themselves slovenly. Still, it can also be an aesthetic decision, favoring the color for how it looks and the selfish enjoyment derived from it. Much to the chagrin of those prone to hasty reaction, the black-suited Satanist cannot be so easily pegged in terms of actual intent.

Those who primarily or exclusive wear black in general can sometimes be read as unapproachable, alien, and, in short, different. But, unlike subculturally defined couture that may also gain this reaction, such as that of blatant neo-Nazis and Klansmen, the donning of the black suit by a known Satanist isn't so easily summarized. Worn by us, the masses may be reminded of what little they know of us, but the fear of uncertainty doesn't necessarily provoke them to negative action (such as it might against avowed racists, goth kids, or metalheads). Chiefly, because they lack a clear definition of what they think wearing black "means" to us and, thus, doesn't permit them the validation given by mainstream backing for any outward admonishment. Because, let's be real here, these types of dismissal or condemnation are more agreeable and enjoyable for the armchair critic if he or she has majority approval and support, be it real or imagined. Their cowardice in not being able to form their own opinion, let alone an accurate one, is all too obvious to those who tread the Left Hand Path.

The ratio of black to non-black can also proffer some interesting outcomes. Taken to a combination closer to a traditional level, the Satanist can move freely through the culture, mindfully exacting the favoritism that the icon of the suit brings. We are certainly not oblivious to the effects of wardrobe on the masses, the way it is perceived and treated. Satanists who take advantage of this particular combination often succeed in their business dealings, make lasting (and useful) impressions on people, and given certain considerations in the public arena that lower-dressed people are not afforded. It's also fair to say that many women find dapper gents incredibly refreshing in light of having to settle for the baseball-cap-and-jeans variety of males.

Tilting the ratio more towards the black (without going all the way) can often result in some desired manipulation. While you are still wearing the respected garb of conventional society, the amount of black can often be perceived as mysterious, or powerful, or attractive. In contrast to countercultural wearers of this color, a wider variety of people will often feel comfortable with your appearance but also enjoy being in the company of someone who stands out just enough to still remain acceptable -- for whatever purpose that company serves. Put simply, the herd don't have to put themselves on the defensive when around this Satanist because, in their minds, we're not "pushing" what some might call "Satanic drag" in their faces -- particular when they're within visual distance of their peers. Honey over vinegar, in this case. And, it's all too apparent how many folks need some sugarcoated guidance sometimes.

The choice of suit also factors in. Many people are under the impression that a suit, any suit, will look good and serve their desired ends. But, like nature itself, quality matters, and your dad's old beat-up polyester suit might not cut it. Believe me, I can spot the man wearing a suit because he has to, the man who thinks wearing any suit is good enough, and the man who wears a suit well and with intent, and know the difference between the three. Remember, folks: Lesser Magic actually requires insight as well as effort.

Knowing all of this, the black suit serves marvelously as a sort of personal stratification device. The braindead sheep who populate music subculture and other desperate groupings of that sort will either dismiss you or steer clear of you, which is advantageous. The "system" will often respect you, respect which can be utilized. Those approaching you for friendship or love who take issue with you (via their associations assumed or derived from your black suit) probably harbor other myopic views and are often not worthy of relationship consideration, which also works out. Each person, depending on their assumptions, values, and level of understanding, will often fall quite willingly into their own self-made pegholes... thanks to a suit. Imagine that.

Not only aren't all folks who wear black Satanists, all Satanists do not wear black, either. Satanists run the gamut of personal fashion, and non-Satanists might never know that they have one of us in their midst. There is power in this as well -- in this case, the power of anonymity, which is a benefit to some Satanists more than others.

And, although this almost goes without saying, the suit is a tool. That is, its purpose is utilization for one or more of the motivations mentioned earlier. It is not a source of identity for the self -- something the herd often can't understand, either in others or themselves. The difference between the suit being an outward projection of your pride and/or utility, and the suit needing to inwardly provide you with purpose or outside affirmation is the difference between the Satanic acceptance of the ego as self-generated and, conversely, the Christian practice of externalizing the ego in hopes of receiving validation from others (in their case, it's usually from a "god"). It's fair to say that some of the herd (often by means of projection) will assume your suit is for identification purposes rather than for utility, and there's power in even that opinion if recognized and used accordingly.

So, where do all of those lovely Satanic Witches figure into the implementation of the black suit, an overwhelmingly male social tool? In the strictest sense, they do not. But, nor do they need to. In addition to merely being of the fairer sex and all that comes with it, women have a much broader range of Lesser Magic attire and trappings within the culture to choose from, and being in a state of well dress is only one of them -- though, certainly a very powerful one in many instances. More on this subject is contained within the pages of *The Satanic Witch* by Anton Szandor LaVey, if further study is desired.

So, listen up, gentlemen! If you've outgrown feeding off the fashion identities of your favorite rock stars or finding inspiration for dress in your nearest dumpster, you might discover that the mindful donning of a good suit unlocks potential power and privilege in Western culture simply unknown or unimagined by the majority of the herd. While others are needlessly complaining that "the system" is keeping them down for the socially-hostile way they dress, you can button up those cuffs, straighten up that tie, and avoid such pointlessly masochistic exercises by, instead, jumping on available archetypes and riding them for all that they are worth. It is a clear and active example of how to avoid viewing the world "as it should be" and how to work within the context of that same world as it really is.

Now, that's undefiled wisdom!

OTHER PEOPLE

Sartre once posited that the source of potential suffering for the individual is other people. Nothing could be closer to the truth. The higher man sees these other people -- the Great Unwashed, the herd masses -- as the primary cause of all unreason, offense, and stagnation. It is the individual's chief aim to inoculate himself against this societal virus, for if left unattended, it would devour him whole.

Other people are the ones who champion the absurd presumption of human equality because it shields them from facing their errors. Apologists, one and all. The myth of equality gives them a semblance of power in lives that have earned none, all the while applauding the inept and denying recognition to the superior in one transparent step.

Other people are destroyers of all that is beauty, replacing it with bland lines, tired textures, and colorless consumerism. They trade knowledge for programming, and then pat themselves on the back for their drone aesthetic. They claim fashionable identities as creative expression, and then hold them mindlessly up to the world as something impressive. And, like some sick inversionist plot, those who do not follow the program are consigned to the label of misfit, malcontent, outsider.

Other people are shortsighted revisionists. They harbor the infantile notion that if they change the terminology, they change the condition. Simple answers for simple people with simple minds. And simply stated, other people do not want to think. But they want the laurels that come with thinking. These are the same people who feel that if they wait long enough for something, they should get it -- like a trained rodent who repeatedly taps the feeder bar and is puzzled when a morsel is not dispensed.

Other people demand what they so delusionally call rights. But what their two-dimensional minds never seem to process is that rights -- true rights -- are never given, they are taken. They confuse rights with legislated privileges. And they are equally occupied with the conceit that governmental dictates constitute law. Rules are not laws. Laws, such as nature has granted us, cannot be broken. Only human constructs can. But don't tell that to other people. They don't want to hear it.

Other people wish to be babysat by their master of choice. But they will never call it such. They rationalize it into convenient jargon such as a god, or concepts of right and wrong, good and evil. They can actually ascribe a universal definition to these man-made guidelines so unquestioningly that they cannot see anything outside of the construct.

Such is the ethic of slaves.

A Night On The Brocken
The Walpurgisnacht Ceremony

Written by Matt G. Paradise - Church of Satan
Copyright 1999 C.E. (XXXIV Anno Satanas)

(Preparation: In addition to those directions of ritual planning prescribed in *The Satanic Bible* by Anton Szandor LaVey, the ritual chamber should be decorated with any and all reminders of spring, be they plants, flowers, or other seasonal items. If incense is used, it should be musky or earthy. If music is used, Mendelssohn's "Walpurgisnacht" or Stravinsky's "The Rite of Spring" are both recommended. This ceremony must only be performed at night on the 30th of April, preferably at 9 p.m. and may be conducted inside or outside. If the latter is chosen, a mountain bonfire with proper clearing would be appropriate.)

(The PRIEST, or CELEBRANT, follows ritual directions from *The Satanic Bible* and then reads its Invocation.)

(Names read:) Mephistopheles! Asmodeus! Lilith! Bast! Ishtar! Naamah! Pan! (Participants repeat each name after it has been said by the Celebrant.)

(CELEBRANT calls forth the Four Princes of Hell from *The Satanic Bible*. Sword is then handed to ACOLYTE and the following is read with arms outstretched.)

CELEBRANT: Rejoice! The end of the Wild Hunt is here and we stand before the veil separating two worlds -- the Between Time. The wolf, with flashing eyes and blood-drenched jaws, now leaves behind his arctic hunting ground and enters the forest fortress of earthiness and fertility that is the grand climax of spring.

We hail to revelry this night, to youth and beauty and strength. We invoke the Black Flame of Satan to guide us to the Infernal bonfires atop the great Brocken, to infuse in us the unending lusts of Pan, and to bring about the Is To Be.

And he who fears these words tonight deserves his chains to wear.

CELEBRANT: Shemhamforash!
PARTICIPANTS: Shemhamforash!

CELEBRANT: Hail Satan!
PARTICIPANTS: Hail Satan!

(Gong is struck; music or other audio, if any, begins)

CELEBRANT: The wind stills and starlight fades as the moon veils her radiant face. From the Pit, a myriad of sparks fly forth as hosts of demons cast their magic-mad over the Earth, extolling the Prince of Darkness whom we for ages know. Amid smoke, the Black Flame rises, gleams and purifies our hearts, while it strikes terror into the minds of the benumbed and the servile.

PARTICIPANTS: Blessed are the bold! Cursed are the sheep!

CELEBRANT: Around the Infernal blaze loom giant oaks, their roots like winding serpents weaving out of rock and earth to swell and unbind, to affright and ensnare our enemies, curious outsiders and pretenders to the throne. For only those who master the labyrinth of flames with serious mind may dwell in the Devil's fane.

PARTICIPANTS: The Earth is ours! To have and to hold!

CELEBRANT: Now is the time for celebration! Now is the hour of flesh and of passion! Forever and ever! World without end!

PARTICIPANTS: We herald the Age of Fire! Strength through joy!
(Gong is struck)

Read the following Keys aloud from *The Satanic Bible*:

> The Second Enochian Key
> The Seventh Enochian Key
> The Thirteenth Enochian Key

(Ringing of the bell as before; music or other audio, if used, fades to out)

CELEBRANT: So it is done!

GREATER THAN SHEEP AM I, AND SMILING

Being a very intuitive person from an exceptionally early age, I simply could not block out the patent inequality amongst my so-called peers. The simple fact that some children are smarter than others, more self-motivated than others, and more in touch with the human condition than others was to be avoided at all costs according to our "educators," who recognize a threat to their frail construct of "good information" and replace reality with the lie of equality. Let's just say that they have due reason to fear the truth. Because it often hurts.

Yet all of these children, as if product on an assembly line, were treated the same by teachers who were, more likely than not, also foil-stamped out by society to obey the popular tenets of mediocrity and mindless worship when they were children. The big difference is that, on real assembly lines, defective merchandise is removed and discarded. Feel free to read into that last statement.

For the years following, the dangerous trend of socially-enforced homogeneity would pass by my eyes and then bombard the minds of the herdlings -- like a looped sequence of the same gruesome car accident. Each instruction, each sugar-coated virus, targeted their fledgling egos with the idea that each and every one of them is supposedly special, important, necessary, and able to contribute to a world of sheep, which they'd soon become. In like a lamb, out like a slave.

In school, we were all treated to this nauseating egalitaria through whitewashed history and one-sided political analysis. "All Men Are Created Equal" wasn't a statement I could mindlessly swallow in good conscience, though I'd find myself alone in this attainment of reason. All of the purported notions of Constitutionally-granted "equality" became indoctrination meant to keep servants in line. And not a servitude deemed by racial selection, but one that includes the mass of automatons who ooze forth from the quagmire of all colors.

So, how is it that I see what few do? Because I, in the majority of ways, am vastly superior to them. And atop my deserved mountain of higher man, I look upon them, with disdainful eyes, and state pridefully and rightfully, "I am better than you."

That's right. Better. Better than the drooling consumerists, the unquestioning worker drones, the media puppets, the God adorers, the devil worshipers, the leftists, the right-wingers, the music subculture-drenched, the hippies, the yuppies, the pathetic New Agers and all of the other pseudo-nature religionists, the censors, the insecure stooge educators of our schools and colleges, and let's not forget all of the losers, posers, inepts, failures, irrational thinkers, irresponsibles, non-committers, lazy, stupid, uncreative, feeble-minded, miscellaneous humans. Trust me, if you're in there, I am probably laughing at you.

Some of the reason for my blatant superiority is due in part to my parents. I am indeed a lifeform created by the conjoining of two individuals' genetic information, as others are, but such similarities with the species largely stop there. I wasn't the bastard spawn of stupid, uncaring, irresponsible social leeches. I was made by rational, extremely intelligent, educated, focused, driven people. As a result, I possess an over-the-scale IQ, started reading by age four, was asked to skip two grades in school, and was generally the intellectual bane of my teachers' existences, constantly catching their improprieties, flaws in logic, and brainwashing techniques. Translation: I was very bright and very bored.

Many people pride themselves on being able to ferret out nonsense and when someone's pulling the wool over their eyes. Throughout my life, I've watched person after person repeatedly chant this astuteness of theirs as if some self-affirming mantra -- but with no considerable sign of it. I could stare at the trap, point the trap out, and even explain what the trap is, but their inferiority wins out over such clarification and they're snagged. One of many reminders that I am not them.

I've also been consistently repelled by group approval, whereas the lessers (and the economy) are pretty much dependent upon it. Much of my childhood was happily spent away from other, more collective-minded children. It brought me great pleasure to play by myself, invent my own worlds, draw my own pictures of how I saw things, and interact with the assortment of imaginary characters and pretend pals who were far more colorful, far more interesting, and infinitely more akin to what

I was about (via the life I gave them) than most of the pint-sized vassals in the outside kingdom. I have exceptionally fond memories of my cherished childhood solitude. As a result, I am even more focused, more independent, and way more self-aware than any of the do-nothings and say-nothings of the world who desperately flip through self-help books in order so that they can look in the mirror and not hate themselves. It must simply feel like a disease not to love yourself and, instead, have to replace that with acceptance from others. I cringe at such an unrelatable prospect.

Considering the group mentality out there, it's not exactly hard to be in a superior position. Most people are as humdrum as they are predictable, and it's obvious that they have little to no desire to elevate themselves in any meaningful way. They aren't stepping outside of their social boundaries, they aren't questioning the rules, they won't break out of their stagnant patterns, and they certainly aren't going to sever the bonds to their self-appointed masters in the near future. Given the majority as a measuring stick, I'd say that my superiority is in no danger of being snuffed out anytime soon.

Of course, the very word "superior" strikes terror into the hearts of many -- so much so that they will enlist even the most desperate logic against it. The more learned of them (and this especially applies to the stereotypical academic types whose reality is only in books and politically-correct college courses) will smugly dismiss the term as being vague and falsely empowering. And, if not qualified, it may very well be that. However, one does not need to throw out this baby with the bathwater, no matter how unpleasant looking he might be. Superiority is subjective, but certainly not invalid. There are objective standards that apply to comparing human thought, behavior, and interaction, and they are all subject to a sliding scale of value and application. This is not a theory or an opinion, but observable fact. The quality of difference is all around us. And it is what separates each and every person on this planet. If you wanted diversity, then here it is!

Naturally, your environment matters as well. The superior person is the one who can adapt and continue to prosper as the cultural landscape shifts and evolves. What remains are those inferior types who fall by the wayside as a result of their narrow-mindedness, solipsism, and over-reliance upon the belief of social stability. As a result of their ill-preparedness, they tacitly consign themselves to being food for the gods, be they corporate, media, or individual. It is as nature decrees.

Superiority can depend upon the situation, but if you find that you often excel and are head and shoulders above most of those around you in a considerable number of very applicable ways, then it's a little tough not to call it what it is. This is not to imply that those below you in performance or intelligence are necessarily useless or of no value. But, there is definitely something terribly wrong with the assertion that all of humanity resides on one stratum of significance, evenly aligned in perfect equality, and free of any distinction. Such delusions are crushed underfoot merely by opening a history textbook.

Satanism offers no quarter for the minions of all-embracing belief systems and universally-inclusive mentalities bent on discounting merit and supporting ineptitude. Such pathetic inversions are a sop for those who refuse to come to grips with the immovable hierarchy inherent to life on Earth. Spiritualists of all stripes have railed against this aspect of the natural order for centuries, and still ham-handedly use chapter and verse (or sutras, or vedas, or even golden tablets) in a vain attempt to drag others -- often, their betters -- down to their make-believe level. Though, something tells me that this hand of cards is getting more difficult to play. Especially when everyone knows the anti-climactic outcome.

TO THE DEVIL HIS DUE

Through time unending, the Devil has remained the highest embodiment of the human spirit. From his mythological expulsion, the worthiest of men can admire his drive and independence -- that passion and perseverance that only a few taste and cherish inextricably. His progeny feel regardless of external dictate, revel without want of approval, and strive in spite of imposition.

The Devil, in all of his forms, provides the human race with an archetype befitting of the self-aware, the one who knows his strengths and harbors no shame in his true individuality. All autonomy begins its gestation in the Black Flame, and maintains itself outside of all popular convention.

The greatest heresy the Devil ever bestowed unto man was the power of doubt, the potent inoculation against all irrationality, unfounded belief, and servitude -- to avoid the common trap of accepting anything at face value and to find knowledge in the most obscured and darkest halls through which all others are so gleefully blind.

True to his name, the Devil has served as mankind's most astute accuser. Through notable figures of human history, he has taken to the task of smashing man's collective delusions and forcing the pendulum to swing back to the position of reason. In the Devil's house, you are not granted your illusions or your safety in numbers. And no God is listening.

The Devil gloriously resides in man's mind, his heart, and his groin. The rolling rhapsody of lust is always in key with the Devil's symphony, and it's an undeniable tune, for it is a part of us all and the reason we exist.

Every viable step of advancement, be it scientific, literary or social, bears his cloven hoofprint, for it is the original mindful rebel whose essence fuels the progress of mankind -- all to the chagrin of the superstitious and the mentally enslaved. Without his example, man would have remained wallowing in the quagmire of ignorance, fear, and developmental paralysis.

Every beat of our hearts is infernal.

And its very bloodline,

eternal.

APPENDIX

I. Essay Source List

"Further Evidence of the Satanic Age" (previously unpublished, 2007)

"Ego Transference and the Herd" (from *Not Like Most* #13, 2003)

"Producer or Consumer? Which One Are You?" (from *Not Like Most* #15, 2005)

"Pop Goes The Pretense" (from *Not Like Most* #12, 2002)

"Absolutes Can Corrupt Absolutely" (from *Not Like Most* #13, 2003)

"Love Is A Many Conditional Thing" (from *Not Like Most* #15, 2005)

"Dating Outside Your Race" (expanded, orig. from *Not Like Most* #10, 2000)

"Let's Hear It For Sexual Objectification" (edited, from *Not Like Most* #6, 1998)

"Absolute Human Companions: A Practical Inquiry" (from *Not Like Most* #14, 2004)

"The Misanthrope's Survival Guide" (edited, from *Not Like Most* #14, 2004)

"The Internet: Tool of Stratification" (previously unpublished, 2007)

"From Out Of The Woodwork" (from *Not Like Most* #13, 2003)

"Sifting The Ashes of Anton LaVey" (from *Not Like Most* #7, 1998)

"Rosemary Revisited: A Satanic Look at One of the Scariest Movies of All Time" (from *Not Like Most* #8, 1999)

"B-Horror Dates To Dismember" (from *Not Like Most* #5, 1997)

"The Satanic Side of the Enlightenment" (from *Not Like Most* #9, 1999)

"Satanism and Racialism: Dividing Lines and Common Ties" (from *Not Like Most* #6, 1998)

"If Voting Changed Anything" (reworked, from Diabologue blog site)

"Everybody's Out To Get Me!" (edited, from *Poo Poo Magazine* #17, 1997)

"Bangin' In Littleton" (from *Not Like Most* #9, 1999)

"Everything I Learned To Hate About People, I Learned In Kindergarten" (reworked and edited, from *Poo Poo Magazine* #17, 1997)

"The Black Suit In Both Theory and Application" (from *Not Like Most* #16, 2007)

"Other People" (previously unpublished, 2002)

"A Night On The Brocken (The Walpurgisnacht Ceremony)" (from *Not Like Most* #10, 2000)

"Greater Than Sheep Am I, And Smiling" (expanded and edited, from *Not Like Most* #10, 2000)

"To The Devil His Due" (previously unpublished, 2001)

APPENDIX

II. COMPOSITE INTERVIEW

[The following excerpts are from interviews I'd granted from the early-1990s until 2007. They have been extracted and arranged in a manner to more properly organize information on myself, Satanism, and other related subject matter. Also, a few of the interviews from which these segments were pulled had not been published until now, and I felt they deserved a better fate than inside a storage file on my computer. Enjoy. - MGP]

Q: What is Purging Talon all about and how did it come to be?

MGP: Previous to official publishing efforts with Purging Talon, I had discovered the world of zines back in 1984 when I had purchased a KISS zine through a small ad in the back of a magazine, which at that time had offered the effective enticement of bootlegged concerts on cassette. (My interest in KISS goes beyond merely being a fan of the music. In my adolescence, they represented both an impressive and groundbreaking visual image as well as a very Satanic life attitude: that of going after what you want in life, even in the face of adversity.) Upon seeing that independent publishing was actually possible, and held more promise than simply marketing bootlegs, I started considering doing one of my own. After a couple of attempts from 1987-1992, both of which were dissolved due to either lack of interest on the part of others or, more especially, on my own, I began to take the idea of publishing a bit more seriously when I had won a computer in the Summer of 1993. On Halloween Night of that year, I released the first issue of *Poo Poo Magazine* and, thus, the birth of Purging Talon Publishing. In addition to a few titles that lived comparatively short lives, such as *DeSade Magazine*, *Slambook*, and *Flames From The Internet*, we have published two magazine titles (*Not Like Most* and *Superhighway To Hell* -- the latter, now an online resource/website), plus we sell videos, promo product items (over 200, at last count), and now books with the debut of *The Book of Satanic Quotations* (first edition). Under the Purging Talon banner, I also produced two public access shows: *Subterranean SINema* and the video version of *Satanism Today*.

Our main print title is *Not Like Most*, which is specifically devoted to Satanism. NLM was first published in the summer of 1995 and we've gone through 12 issues, with a new one due out early in 2003. Serving as the primary outlet for my own writing, NLM was the one title that not only survived the decline of zine popularity in the mid-90s when our other titles (as well as those of others) did not, but also has surpassed the best days of those former titles.

One before-the-fact trivia item that many people don't know about NLM: I fought for many months through 1995 with the title of the magazine. Chiefly, because I wanted to come up with a title that wasn't necessarily predictable. Though I respect those mag titles that express a more religious connotation, I wanted to come up with something that summed up the philosophical end of our religion -- that to which I was personally receptive. A friend of mine was in the room, and his contribution was something to the tune of "So... you're doing a mag on Satanism... obviously you need to come up with a title that captures Satanism... well, I'll tell you something... you Satanists are certainly unlike a whole lot of people." To which I said, "Oh, we're definitely not like most... WAITAMINUTE!!!" And with that exclamation came the name of the mag.

Q: On April 30, 2002, you published *The Book of Satanic Quotations*. Could you tell us more about this publication?

MGP: TBoSQ is the first official book release from Purging Talon. Two years in the making, spanning over five centuries and over 250 authors, it's a collection of quotes that truly resonates with the Satanic philosophy. I suppose I got tired of thumbing through books of quotations that really didn't reflect my religious and philosophical viewpoint, and more than realizing that the mass of the ones in major circulation are well-slathered with Christianized thinking and sentiments in clear violation of Satanic discrimination and insight. So, like the impetus to many of the things I produce, I decided that since the world didn't have a certain item of media in it that measured up to my standards or didn't jibe with my vision, then I had to create it myself, if just to have a copy for myself. Upon meeting and getting to know many of the more media-minded and creation-motivated Satanists over the past two decades, I find that I am often enough not alone in that want.

Q: Why did you start *Subterranean SINema*?

MGP: I got my first taste of public access television in early-1995 when I was the guest on a show called *Cross Currents*, a largely political op-ed show. I discussed the 10 points of The Contract With The American Family, which the then-existing Christian Coalition was whoring to the media and government at the time. I enjoyed the experience enough to want to do my own show. Upon getting into the production end of television, I was inspired by yet another form of media, and then went to school for it -- which culminated in a Bachelors degree in Communications. In addition to working in network television, doing the rare moment of video documentary work (which I would like to do more of in the future), and producing SubSIN as well as a new show for VCAM Channel 15 (public access), I'm well occupied and find video a welcome and complimentary addition to my media endeavors.

When initially coming up with ideas for a show between 1995-1997, I was brainstorming with some associates on creating a show called *Poo Poo TV* (patently connected to the magazine, which at that point already had a radio show I did one-half of called *Poo Poo Radio*). It was to be an experiment in guerilla video, something along the lines of what would surface a few years later as *The Tom Green Show* on MTV. The idea fell through, largely due to incompetence on the parts of all but myself and one Vanilla Christ. At that point, I chose to abandon the main idea and work on another. Through all of that came *Subterranean SINema* and the video terrorism that had transpired over its seven seasons (as of 2003).

Why did I do the show? A few reasons: 1) I want to see something on TV that I actually want to watch, 2) it serves as the most receptive medium to transmit ideas, concepts, and people whom I feel are underrepresented, and 3) its existence obliquely promotes my other endeavors.

The first episode of SubSIN was dedicated to Anton LaVey, a true showman and a real inspiration for my creation of the program.

Q: It's obvious that the media is your forte. Why did you follow this particular path?

MGP: Ever since I was little, I was fascinated by many aspects of media, particularly in the area of media production. Many of my childhood projects -- if I could call them such -- were specifically geared towards creative media: music, art, theater, writing, etc. As I got older, I developed my various interests in media, gained professional experience in them, and found that I could profit from being a jack of all media trades. And that kind of diversity is extremely importance in this business, as well as having the talent and ability to round up diverse experience and focus it into viable projects. So, along with being able to do media well, I also enjoy it and have a real passion for my work. Sometimes, that throws people a little, perhaps thinking that Purging Talon is all about either money or merely a profitable hobby for me, and then hearing me discuss the things I create with a great deal of enthusiasm and passion. In many of such conversations, I've been told that I talk about Purging Talon the way proud parents discuss their children. In many respects, I do feel a strong tie to my work, and I feel that the pride and effort put into it is recognized and appreciated by not only its fanbase but by focused, driven, and creative people to whom I can relate -- perhaps, an extension of the "mutual admiration society" idea which the Church of Satan itself also practices.

Q: When did you discover *The Satanic Bible*?

MGP: Oddly enough, I discovered *The Compleat Witch* first when I was 13. I had read it, read into it, and understood on a very intuitive level that I was a Satanist. I found *The Satanic Bible* a couple of years later in a great old used bookstore (which, like many good things, was cleared away for some random den of consumerism). I wasn't really searching for anything in the way of religion, and had been pretty much disgusted by what served as its prime examples by the age of 12. But, the cover and the name looked evocative and I had an initial introduction to LaVey from TCW, so I bought it, read it, and upon remembering what I'd read from the author previously, put it all together and realized that the title of Satanist seems all the more fitting.

Of course, this was the 1980s: the era of rampant fundamentalist Christianity, the Reagan Era, and all of that, so it was an interesting time to be a very "out" Satanist and a teenager between 1980-1988. For those who weren't both at the time (or simply don't recall), it was a very irrational time, one in which being just another sheep was at its most socially applauded. Those screwy talk shows that (luckily) had Church of Satan members or Satanists as guests were all too representative of the gestation of Satanic Panic -- particularly, the audiences, who appeared to be in high mob mentality state (and I mean "high" in the narcotic metaphor sense). Needless to say, it was also an enlightening time for mindful teen rebellion and, more importantly, for learning the lessons of the herd. Lest we forget...

Q: How long did it take for you to join the Church of Satan?

MGP: I had considered it back in 1984, but I didn't have the address. In 1989, when *The Satanic Witch* was released, I then had the address but decided to wait until I felt I had something to contribute to the organization. After a stint in numerous bands, I went back to school for a short time, and had decided that broadcasting was definitely a field to explore. Once having that end of my life solidified, I then joined the Church of Satan in 1991 and thus became a member.

Q: When did you become a Priest in the Church of Satan?

MGP: The Priesthood was granted to me in March of 1997.

Q: How in 40 years is it that we are still termed "devil worshipers who sacrifice children" when proof exists to the contrary?

MGP: Truth be known, I really don't hear much of this accusation in modern day, and particularly when compared to the 1980s "Satanic Panic" era. If a minority of folks are still dredging up tabloid news and outdated fundamentalist Christian propaganda, then perhaps their adherence to belief denies even the fact that the FBI debunked all of the "Satanic Ritual Abuse" nonsense in the early-1990s. Belief is powerful in that weak-minded people find a false sense of empowerment through avoiding the facts and putting their unquestioned trust in something outside of themselves. And this extends beyond conventional religion, reaching into other areas such as politics, pop culture, sex, ethics, etc.

Some of these same weak-minded individuals, by having no real personal power in their lives, find it necessary to invent an enemy to battle against, fulfilling a sense of purpose that they cannot (or will not) achieve in their real lives. Perhaps, their idea of "Satan" serves that purpose -- certainly not a new observation as Dr. LaVey covered some of this in *The Satanic Bible*. And if they have convinced themselves so thoroughly that we, as agents of the Devil, simply must fit the image of what they need us to be, then the illusion might feel more grounded by having a less figurative representation to rail against.

Belief is the negation of fact. Moreover, the believer must shut out all reason and evidence to keep the illusion of belief alive. Otherwise, it's back to having to face the real world and the reality of carnal existence -- a scary proposition for the inept, the lazy, or the stupid. All advancement in cultural evolution throughout world history has occurred in opposition to spiritual belief systems. Conversely, all obstacles in the way of this advancement have, at their core, the influence of these same belief systems behind them.

Q: Do you feel the principles of Satanism are timeless and flexible enough to withstand evolution of societies?

MGP: Satanists (and, hence, Satanism) will always exist. In fact, by other names or no name at all, Satanism has been an operative force throughout human history -- because it is an eternal reminder that existence is purely carnal. It is a fact that the laws of nature do not require approval; they operate regardless of how they are perceived. Satanists recognize this fact, unfettered by pipe-dreams of how things "should be." Therefore, the caprice and timeliness of a society's views are inconsequential. Nature is not listening, nor is any sort of "god."

Satanic forces already rule the world. Only time and intelligence will tell whether or not people become tired of their distractions and fantasies, and acknowledge what remains once belief is abandoned. If not, then we as Satanists will proceed as we always have -- ever forward, and to live our lives to their fullest.

Q: Can *Lex Talionis* be slowly worked into the mainstream despite people's fear and misconceptions of Satanism?

MGP: *Lex Talionis* isn't exactly a foreign concept for people. When the attacks on 9/11 occurred in the United States, the majority of Americans were not crying out for forgiveness -- they were wanting justice. Whether or not people get over their misconceptions of Satanism isn't reliant upon formally accepting *Lex Talionis* because the latter is already built into our carnal natures. For the herd, they are allowed to be perceived as separate issues. However, those who are able to look beyond belief and investigate this concept will find that it is nothing new, that it has been with us for millennia, and that Satanism is its primary champion in modern times. But, since the "mainstream" is comprised of folks on various levels of learning and ability to learn, the outcomes will vary.

Q: If one were to conduct a broad survey of Americans asking them to describe a "typical Satanist," what sort of portrait would emerge?

MGP: In many instances, I'm sure a false image of who and what Satanists are would surface. With the advent of the Internet, though, it's possible that a clearer picture is garnered, particularly from the youth, who by and large may not remember the days of Satanic Panic or other misleading propaganda. Still, other people have no idea what Satanism is about and have probably never thought about it. Though, some of the old false descriptions may still be out there: that we're devil worshippers, that Satanism is a teen phase, that it's tied to metal music more than anything else, that it's "inverse Christianity" and therefore dismissible, etc. The criminal behavior that others have attempted to wrongly align us with seems to be a correlation on the decline.

It would be fair to say, however, that I don't overtly or even emotionally concern myself with how others perceive my religion. Rather, I keep a pragmatic eye upon situations that may affect my life negatively, but those are few and far between. I'm not looking for blind acceptance, and I'm certainly not competing for the good graces of total strangers. If people want the information, it's out there. If people don't want it and wish to entertain their delusions of what they think it is, then that's going to be the case no matter how pervasive the availability of information on Satanism is.

Most people seem to enjoy their ignorance. They are often most comfortable wearing the proverbial blinders through life and feel discomfort when presented with the truth. And, many of them never want to admit when they are wrong and have been misled, so the comfortable lie is held onto all the more. Moreover, many of these same people feel a great deal of contrived power from having a self-appointed "bad guy" to rail against, whether it be a devil, a politician, another religion, a race of people, etc. For them to accept the reality of Satanism would disafford them that cherished paper tiger, putting them into the uncomfortable position of having to place the blame for their life's struggles on their actual source -- oftentimes, themselves.

Q: Does CoS pursue political and social purposes?

MGP: Within the Church of Satan, we have members of all political stripes: democrats, libertarians, fascists, monarchists, etc. The reason for such diversity is that, although Satanism defines a common foundation of which Satanists agree, upon that is built the "Is-To-Be" of each individual Satanist. Each Satanist contemplates his or her environment and then finds the political or social means which allow for maximum achievement and freedom. Knowing this, it's safe to say that of the Satanists who involve themselves in the political process (and some don't, by the way), the overwhelming majority of them are voting pragmatically -- for issues, and not "personalities."

Q: As a Satanist, have you felt increasingly threatened or nervous with the advent of the current vocally evangelical Christian White House administration?

MGP: Not at all, but that's just my position on it. And it's a far cry from the 1980s Satanic Panic era. To a relevant degree, we live in better times. 25 years ago, a president like Bush Jr. would have been welcomed unconditionally by the vast majority. And the resulting policies would have been largely unchallenged. People ask more questions these days, and the existence of the Internet fuels that, as well as exposes people to a greater amount of information than two decades back -- not just on Satanism, but on everything. Since the youth picked up on the Internet and seem to use it the most, it's no longer unusual to find a 14 year old kid with a working knowledge of Satanism and his or her 45 year old dad who's completely in the dark on the subject. With the passing of the years, the population continues to educate itself further through greater access to information and is finding that technology and science hold far more validity than outdated myth-based religions. Those are our youth, whose numbers constitute the rising tide of, for example, atheism in modern day. There are people who don't want to see that, but it is so obvious that the youth culture is leaving dead mythologies behind in search of earthly exploits. The evidence of this cultural shift is everywhere, and heavily supported by current authors such as Howard Bloom, Richard Dawkins, and Sam Harris.

What we're seeing now in American culture is that Christianity is in its death throes. Like any ideology in its last days, it's done its best to make the most noise before it expires. This doesn't mean that spirituality or the needing of a master for some is going away. Most likely, the concept of a "god" will be replaced with something else, perhaps media created, if that already isn't the case.

Q: If you consider all of the stereotypes you've observed being imposed on Satanists, which ones might hold more truth than others?

MGP: The popular stereotypes are often so far off the mark, they don't even apply. A minority of people -- the ones who have a better but still incomplete grasp on Satanism -- are prone to knee-jerk reactions to our literature that more simple-minded people never even see. These include accusations of being "fascists" (by whatever trendy definition that overused buzzword holds for any one person), that we're playing a Christian game because of our use of the name Satan (which is not the sole property of Christianity, and even has pre-Judaic roots), that we're "as bad as the rest of them" because we call Satanism a religion (even if it's a religion of the self), or that it *can't* be a religion because there is no deity worship (even if certain schools of Buddhism, as well as Taoism and Confucianism, also share our lack of deity belief/worship).

Q: What sorts of things do you think most people would be surprised to learn about Satanism?

MGP: Where do I begin?! Let's try here...

 A: Satanists have a deep respect for children and animals, both of whom are closer to their animal nature and have yet to be perverted into mindless automata. Also, in my experience, the children of Satanists I personally know are some of the most brilliant, observant, creative, questioning youngsters I know. They certainly are not sheep.
 B: Our strong Law and Order position. In a culture still dealing with the remaining vestiges of Christian influence, Satanists see that true justice has suffered greatly from this opposing force. We champion the concept of *Lex Talionis*: let the punishment fit the crime. The last 10+ years have seen our police forces muzzled by political correctness, sensitivity training, and other counterproductive measures that have served to tie their hands more than anything. The overapplication of rehabilitative efforts on criminals (even violent ones) who, as a result, are allowed to manipulate the system and are beyond reproach truly illustrates the madness of Christian forgiveness.
 C: How much philosophy Satanism contains. While others might like to dismiss Satanism for being a fad or a music subculture thing, Satanism has a lot of meat to it. Our religious philosophy has pulled the carnal truth from a number of sources including Nietzsche, Jung, Mencken, Rand, Milton, Twain, and still others. Even in modern day, there are a number of literary sources that take a very Satanic approach to life, even if they themselves are not Satanists or align themselves with Satanism: Florence King, William A. Henry III, Paul Fussell, Eric Hoffer, and the list goes on.
 D: The whole "devil worship" thing. Forty years of incontrovertible evidence via our literature still doesn't hold a candle to this misconception for some. And it's not only fueled by more predictable sources like Christianity, but also by the Wiccan/Pagan/New-Age crowd. In their attempts to win a Goodguy Badge from society, some of them elevate

themselves in some of their literature by pegging us as "the bad guys." It usually goes to the tune of, "Oh, we're Wiccans and we don't kill animals or commit crimes or worship a devil... like those Satanists!" There is a real victim culture in many of their circles, and a desperate desire to appear "normal" by erroneous contrast with us. You'd think they'd know better.

Q: To apply the name of Satan to this church, implies a connection to the Bible. What is the stance of the CoS on these popular tales and predictions? Who is Christ to the CoS?

MGP: We take the name Satan in concept only, and one boldly and unrepentantly defined by us. Any other connection is thrust upon us by anxious, ignorant, and/or misinformed people. The archetype itself, by whatever name is appropriate, is far older than Christianity or Judaism, and it was these religions that, in order to gain a foothold in the world, decided to destroy and bastardize the 'pagan gods.' Satan has generally been the character who has challenged sterile thought, encouraged indulgence, rebelled against slavery, and truly represented human nature and all that the world offers. By extension, instead of worshiping Satan, we recognize ourselves in this archetype and take up His name.

The Christian Bible was probably one of the greatest pieces of propaganda in world history but, quite frankly, a scientifically, philosophically, and technologically advanced civilization should logically cease to have a need for such outmoded parables and slave ethics. But, seeing as insecurity never goes out of style, those in need seek their babysitters in whatever avenue is acceptable; in LaVey's words, the "privileged lie."

Many Satanists also view the Christian Bible as singular examples of mankind's willing hypocrisy, incompetence, and spinelessness. Jesus Christ is the paradigm for these qualities. How can anyone with human insight and reasonable logic skills accept the phrase "the meek shall inherit the Earth" without laughing? History certainly doesn't support this assertion. From my experience, many people who call themselves Christians are so merely by convenience or unchecked familial influence and not so much by a rational decision, if rationale is possible. It's a truly insecure philosophy that demands its tenets to be installed in humans from early childhood, because if it was introduced for the first time to adults, many would raise their collective eyebrow in suspicion and disgust. Many Christians I've met haven't even read their Bible (at least, not critically), but keep the book on their coffee tables to appear "righteous." And, some just skip the sanguine parts. Many of them really seem to get off on their religion, the self-righteousness feeds their impoverished egos. As trivial as it seems, it's a glaring metaphor for Christianity in general, a mass of contradictions, and almost Freudian.

Q: Do you see the victory of true Satanism over false Satanism as primarily a result of information supremacy?

MGP: Not really. Satanism stands above its imitators largely because of what it represents and because it does this competently. Many of the *ersatz* Alien Elite represent nothing more than parrots of LaVey's published phrases while trying to burn him in effigy at the same time; most likely, to mitigate their guilty consciences. Our detractors spend far too much time and paper lambasting us because they can't be what we are and, often enough, can't become anything at all, save a rabblerouser. Real Satanists show their superiority by their thoughts and actions, not by how well they can commit lines from *The Satanic Bible* to memory. Intelligence and performance above mimicry and incompetence.

Q: Why do goths and Wiccans seem to have such a fascination with Satanism despite their feigned disinterest?

MGP: In all fairness, I'd say that not all involved in the gothic subculture or the religion of Wicca display this behavior, but on equal footing, there is a sizable number that does. In the case of those who do, the motives vary. An obscene majority of Wiccans have a difficult time separating or delimiting the archetype of Satan from the religion of Christianity since it is drilled into their heads through their literature that Satanism is devil worship, and that LaVey's material should be avoided at all costs since they actually might find it more fascinating than the veiled Christian thinking often pandered in many of their tomes. This might explain some of the seemingly bipolar behavior, and even their strange attraction to the Satanism areas online, for example. Blanche Barton wrote an adequate two-part article on the topic of Wicca in two subsequent issues of the Church of Satan publication, *The Cloven Hoof*, so I point those interested in that direction and spare all the repetition.

Those in the goth subculture are often similar in their approach to Satanism in that they too can be vulnerable to their own internally-perpetuated misconceptions of us. But, there is also some resentment from both camps when it comes to the criticism we've leveled at them.

Q: Are you familiar with the church burnings in Norway in the early 1990s at the hands of black metal bands? Would this sort of behavior be approved of by your church?

MGP: Not at all. The Church of Satan takes a strong law and order position in matters such as these, and always has. Criminal action amongst our membership largely results in expulsion as such behavior does not represent our philosophy of "responsibility to the responsible." It could also be said that those who resort to destroying such buildings are often too inept and powerless to rise above their obviously harbored issues with Christianity and, not facing such a reality, succumb to knee-jerk reaction and juvenile vandalism which, by and large, has no effect and would probably make their self-appointed problems worse. If these scofflaws took even a portion of the energy they expend in their so-called "blasphemies" and actually applied it to success and human potential, then perhaps many of us wouldn't view them as tantrum-prone malcontents. To contrast, we as Satanists are masters of our lives, whereas the devil worship/church burning types are slaves to their counter-productive and life-draining hatred of a religion that, if examined, really should have nothing to do with their lives.

Q: How do you feel about LaVey worship?

MGP: It depends a great deal on what you mean by "worship" (not to confuse it with respect or admiration) and how far it goes. Maybe some people are too pathetic and inept to bear the mantle of godhood, so they latch onto a strong, father figure type such as LaVey unintentionally provides them. But, like clockwork, these sad sacks usually journey somewhere else after a profound embarrassment period; often to Wicca or the gothic subculture. They get a lot of our rejects.

Sometimes, the Satanic neophyte is an adolescent who doesn't fit the previous bill but just has a lot of enthusiasm for Satanism and its complete conformity to who and what that teenager is. With these teens, you could possibly end up with some of the most productive and brilliant adult Satanists. Am I talking about myself to a degree? Sure. When I discovered Satanism and had enough time to really process the philosophy, I considered LaVey a role model. And, it's slowly becoming evident that as the years pass, even I have become a sort of role model for some Satanic youth. Maybe that's why I have a slight patience with adolescents. Like the initial over-interest in Greater Magic we often see in youth, we all need to go through certain steps; otherwise we'd never evolve. So, with that, it's often wise to keep the age of the person in mind. The end result is that individuals prove just how committed to Satanism they are juxtaposed with what they accomplish and contribute. And you just can't fake that for very long.

Q: Do you think the sense of humor present in your magazine turns off a lot of overly "evil" people?

MGP: I hope so, if I get your meaning. If by "evil" people, you are referring to those folks who try to make manifest outsiders' twisted interpretations of Satanism, then I say farewell. Don't let the door slam you on the way out. If you (also?) mean those who feel that Satanism should be about enforcing some straitlaced seriousness at all times, then they are also welcomed to exit at any time. Unfortunately, there will always be those moving through our ranks who have the proverbial pitchfork up their behinds. I'm not here to tell them to be otherwise because unless they are loved ones of mine or people I generally care about, I could generally care less. Recently, I've been amassing a small but growing collection of B-grade devil worship movies because I think they're really funny (just like my affection for devil-themed curios and extreme Christian propaganda publishing efforts). Oh, the *horror*! How dare I? Why haven't I had my Priesthood yanked from me? If it was up to the "stuffed robe" types of the world, I'd probably be hanged for lack of solemnity... you get the point.

Q: Was there any possibility of creating a "Church of Satan" with-

out Anton LaVey?

MGP: Considering that Dr. LaVey founded the Church of Satan, the first legally established Satanic church and the first organization in world history to codify Satanism as a philosophy and a religion, I would say no. By that alone, his contribution was beyond significant, it was necessary. But, for those who may misconstrue the Church of Satan as a mere cult of personality, they'd be disappointed to find out that the Church of Satan abhors and condemns the "follower" mentality, instead praising those who make the mindful decision to align with Satanism. Put simply, the true Satanist reads *The Satanic Bible* and sees himself reflected in it. The mere follower type tries vainly to be what the book represents. In the first, we have alignment. In the last, a pseudo-Satanist.

Q: The life of LaVey was a mystery. Who was he actually?

MGP: Much of LaVey's life is transcribed in his biography, *The Secret Life Of A Satanist* by Blanche Barton, as well as some supplementary material in *The Church of Satan* by the same author. However, a more direct gauge of the man may be found in his more personal writings contained in his books, *The Devil's Notebook* and *Satan Speaks!*. Therein, you'll find a witty, sarcastic, insightful, and irreverent gent who didn't suffer fools lightly (if at all), who didn't waste anyone's time saying it like it isn't, and all the while, maintaining an appreciation for the people in his life who really mattered. For me, he was a true and mindfully approached role model. I am proud to be an official of an organization which upholds my standards and counts among its members some of the most impressive and outstanding individuals I know.

Q: You stated in a few interviews that you feel like a "role model" for younger Satanists. Do you still feel like that or has your opinion changed?

MGP: The only way that it has really changed is that it has become more apparent as I get older. Being almost 34 now (2002), I've now met and experienced young Satanists, either Church of Satan members or not, who have grown up during the time of my various works of a public nature. I think it's very heartening specifically when those individuals have taken that admiration and used it as a springboard towards their own autonomous efforts. Fandom and blind adoration only go so far, but in Satanism, it's about what you DO and not how well you can affect the tenets of Satanism without any substantive evidence. I know at least one Satanist in particular (I won't name him here) who has cited me as a role model, but then went on to build and elevate his efforts to a level worthy of respect and admiration -- yes, even *my* respect and admiration, which doesn't come easily. That, to me, is "Satanism in action." I felt very inspired as a youngster of the 1980s reading what Dr. LaVey had written, but I didn't sit around and let such good information fester -- I went out and did something with it and, through such, discovered by own Black Flame, something that's truly mine and representative of my own Godhood. If I serve that capacity in a young Satanist to get out there and excel in their respective fields of strength, then that's something I consider worth recognizing.

Q: Do you feel any need now in a strong and charismatic leader?

MGP: Although I don't believe that anyone could replace Dr. LaVey on this planet on any level, Magus Gilmore has earned the respect and admiration of many through his various pursuits, his media representation, writings, and overall intelligence and insight. And I find no reservation in stating that he is the most natural choice to lead this organization well into the 21st century.

Q: Who are the most important individuals alive?

MGP: Those from whom you have profoundly learned or been inspired, who live a lifestyle and have accomplished their potential despite herd opposition. Each Satanist will gravitate to his or her own set of innovators and motivators, depending on personal taste and goals; though, some common Satanic factors will be present throughout. As for my own list, I'd certainly be at the top of it. After me, the list would probably be brief. Charles Manson once said that he has no dead heroes, but most of the folks I've admired are indeed that: deceased. So, I'd be hard pressed to come up with a sizable list of living ones at this point, given the de-evolution we have been witnessing in the West and the general expendability of the human majority.

Q: Tell us one thing that would surprise us about Matt Paradise.

MGP: Since most people only see my professional side through my media creations, they might miss the fact that I have an enormous capacity for fun. And it's a little sad that some of the more militantly serious Satanists miss out on that in their own lives. Frankly, I feel it would benefit many of them -- particularly the younger ones -- to take much of the energy given to what they don't like in their culture, be it Christianity, herd thought, or mindless political distractions, and channel some of that into what makes The Great Indulgence worthwhile, which is having fun and enjoying life. Certainly, I find merit in deep intellectual discussions and, less often, "talking" Satanism, but there are plenty of times when spontaneous and out-of-the-ordinary activities are the order of the day. As I've heard so many times, that surprises people about me, and in a good way. But, then again, what kind of Satanist would I be if I didn't keep my audience on its toes?

APPENDIX

III. SATANISM FAQ

[This document is the standard informational sheet on Satanism available on the Internet, written by myself. This is version 3.1 and is subject to revision when necessary. - MGP]

What is Satanism?

Satanism, the first carnal religion in human history, was codified and established by Anton Szandor LaVey (1930-1997) with the founding of the Church of Satan in 1966 C.E. (Year One). It is a religion and a philosophy based on man as he really is: a carnal being free from the fiction that is spirituality and one who champions total responsibility, pragmatism, and the here-and-now. Currently, the Church of Satan is headed by High Priest Peter H. Gilmore, High Priestess Peggy Nadramia, and Magistra Blanche Barton. Additional information on Church of Satan hierarchical structure, policies, updates, and more can be found at the Church of Satan's official website: www.churchofsatan.com.

    Satanism has been referred to as an "unreligion" in the sense that it does not subscribe to the notion of an anthropomorphic deity and, by extension, some being who must be worshiped, its most common misconception. Others say that Satanism is challenging popular notions of how "religion" is defined, not content with the dictates of Judeo-Christian strictures. Both are valid opinions. But for those who feel that deity worship and religion must be and always have been inextricably bound, it should be noted that Satanism's lack of deity belief and deity worship is not singular as Buddhism, Confucianism, and Taoism (all considered religions the world over) also share this viewpoint. Also, the concept of a literal "Satan" which infiltrates people's lives and influences their decisionmaking is exclusively Christian, and decidedly not Satanic.

Satanism is further described as being a *de facto* personality type as, in the words of Anton LaVey, "Satanists are born, not made." To try is to lie. It takes a certain set of predispositions to accurately label oneself a Satanist, to naturally feel at home with all that Satanism entails. Satanism, as a philosophy, can be potentially taken and learned from by a large percentage of the population, but this does not make one a Satanist, but, perchance, Satanic. Qualities such as cowardice, insecurity, self-loathing, drug addiction, stupidity, constant life failures, unconditional niceness, and lack of direction (and there are MANY more) are clear indicators that the person in question and the title of Satanist are NOT compatible. For such a person, Satanism isn't a direct reflection of one's core (as it is with Satanists), it can only be a human improvement program at best, which is valid on that level only. This is one distinction that many, be they Satanic "hopeful" or earnest researcher, would be better off to recognize.

It must be stressed that critically reading *The Satanic Bible* by Anton Szandor LaVey is tantamount to understanding at least the basics of Satanism. It is the definitive tome of Satanism and cannot be avoided if accurate knowledge of Satanism is desired. As supplement (read: not replacement), perusing some of the Satanic magazines published by Church of Satan members and officials will lend some insight into Satanism in motion, as a productive model. And of course, websites published by these same folks (including myself) are also useful. Conversely, we do not officially advocate chat rooms and message boards as viable sources of Satanic information.

Membership in the Church of Satan is completely voluntary and not required in order to be a Satanist.

Who is Satan?

In Satanism, Satan is an archetype, a representation of certain qualities that the Satanist embodies including rational self-interest, avoidance of oppressive mentalities, the questioning of all, and a perseverance towards success and human potential. *The Satanic Bible* encapsulates this iconography in The Nine Satanic Statements, which are thus:

1) Satan represents indulgence, instead of abstinence!
2) Satan represents vital existence, instead of spiritual pipe dreams!

3) Satan represents undefiled wisdom, instead of hypocritical self-deceit!
4) Satan represents kindness to those who deserve it, instead of love wasted on ingrates!
5) Satan represents vengeance, instead of turning the other cheek!
6) Satan represents responsibility to the responsible, instead of concern for psychic vampires!
7) Satan represents man as just another animal, sometimes better, more often worse than those that walk on all-fours, who, because of his divine spiritual and intellectual development, has become the most vicious animal of all!
8) Satan represents all of the so-called sins, as they all lead to physical, mental, or emotional gratification!
9) Satan has been the best friend the church has ever had, as he has kept it in business all these years!

Inherently, the Satanic archetype is far more diverse than the limited Christian interpretation -- the name/word is notably pre-Christian: from the Hebrew, meaning "adversary", "opposer" or "one who questions" (and the Jewish "Satan" differs sharply from the Christian one in many ways). Even its etymology is traced back through sources previous to its Hebrew version, from *Shaitan* (Persian) all the way back to *Set* (Egyptian). Satanism, to one degree or another, embraces additional cultural and religious ideas, concepts and imagery such as those of ancient Rome and ancient Greece, Zoroasterism, Asatru, Aztec, Hindu and a multitude of others. We also find the Satanic persona emanating from some or all of the literary works of Milton, Nietzsche, Mencken, Maugham, Twain, Rand, Jung, and many more.

Where can I find an online version of *The Satanic Bible*?

The Satanic Bible is a copyrighted work. Portions may be used in quotations or used for educational purposes (such as the Fair Use laws of the United States dictate), but there is some hefty litigation potentially awaiting the fool who offers the entire tome electronically. LaVey's death also does not negate this copyright: the work is secured until, at the very soonest, 2047 C.E. Obtaining a copy of TSB is not difficult as there are numerous online booksellers that sell the basic Satanic texts, and many offline bookstores -- either independent or of the chain-store variety -- who either stock them or will special order them for customers who make the effort to inquire. Collectively, there are so many sellers of Church of Satan-approved books worldwide with so many shipping and payment options that there is no excuse (and we've heard them all) for not being able to legally acquire or purchase them. If you come across a site that is illegally posting portions or whole versions of Church of Satan books, please report them to the Church of Satan. At this point, Avon/HarperCollins and Feral House (the publishers) as well as the Internet Service Provider hosting it will all be contacted and action may be taken on a legal level. Noncompliance with removal of this material can result in the loss of the webmaster's account.

What is the difference between Satanism and devil worship?

Satanism and devil worship are two distinctly different animals. Devil worship is what it is: the worship of an external deity (in this case, a "devil"), much as it could be labeled inverse Christianity -- that is, confining yourself to the Christian religion and overall model, but merely choosing the "bad guy" in their Bible instead of the purportedly central character. The Satan in Satanism is an archetype, one many know by name and is relative to the culture. Some Satanists choose different aspects of this archetype, depending on geography or just plain aesthetics, but the same characteristics still hold true. It would make little sense for us to claim to embody the archetypal qualities of Satan (rebellion, rational self-interest, carnality, etc.) on one hand, and then attempt to worship an anthropomorphic Satan on the other. In laymen's terms, it's hardly rebellious to worship a figure that represents rebellion. The Satanist finds unproductive and one-sided idol worship to be draining and useless (not to mention hypocritical). Much of this is aptly covered in *The Satanic Bible*.

Are all of those atrocious and illegal acts people say you commit true?

The Church of Satan harshly frowns upon the commission of any illegal act. If you choose to do so, you do it of your own volition and without the approval and consent of the Church of Satan. That is free will and it has consequences. We have stated since the inception that Satanism has nothing to do with animal or human sacrifice (the top of page 89 of *The Satanic Bible* states this in black and white, quite clearly). Likewise, we are against child molestation because we hold children in such high regard, seeing them as natural magicians, beings much closer to their nature than most of the consumer-programmed adults out there. If a Church of Satan member is convicted of a serious crime, particularly a violent one and one that violates the tenets of Satanism, that person's membership is often revoked. And, yes, we have kicked people out of the CoS.

If you don't believe in an actual Satan, then why do you say "Hail Satan" in texts and rituals?

In addition to what is stated before considering how we contextualize Satan, this is my take on this fairly common question:

1) "Hail Satan!" (the exclamation point is optional, though preferred) is often another way of saying "Hail Me!" Since we Satanists embody the qualities of the archetype of Satan, it stands to reason that the phrase is both apropos and analogous. You very well could say "Hail Me!" instead, but keep in mind this...

2) "Hail Satan!" is also a salute to our achievements (both collective and, more importantly, individual), ethics, and heritage. It is a statement of pride in defiance of a polyglot, egalitarian, and ignorant way of life represented by the nauseating Christ ethic and its followers. If we have signed any pact with Satan, it is this.

What do you mean by "Alien Elite"?

We use the phrase, "Alien Elite" to describe ourselves. Often, it is the shortsightedness of people that disallows them to comprehend what this phrase means, even if they've read all of our books, magazines, and websites. Typically, they skip the word "alien." A big mistake, considering that it is an important modifier in the term. What it means is that we, as Satanists, are largely alien in the society at large: we do not generally subscribe to the disposable, consumer-obsessed culture that others do, our issues are different, the stands we take are often neither right nor left but something else entirely (one aspect of what we refer to as The Third Side), we question everything in a world that mostly goes along with established thought and rarely inquires as to how or why, and we simply represent something that most do not -- all of this is in step with the archetype of Satan which we embrace. And we also embrace this alienation. By living such a pure and undiluted life, we are, in many ways, better than most of the human sheep. By being a minority (and we will always be a minority due to the laws of nature -- she simply does not give all of her gifts to all people) and possessing pragmatic and forward-thinking values that are above the interest of the masses, plus adding the intellect and instinct, the creativity and the resourcefulness, and all of those qualities reflected in our books, we are indeed the Alien Elite.

Anton LaVey is merely ripping off other philosophers.

Extremely limited (and limiting) thinking, indeed. When LaVey refers to an idea, concept, or quote derived or taken from someone else, he often cites the author, either in the paragraph or in the indices of his books. If anything LaVey writes seems or is similar to past concepts, oftentimes, it is augmented with modern circumstances, his own thoughts, and is analogous to our philosophy. Seeing that Satanism is a work in progress, something like science meets philosophy, we are fully justified in choosing the concepts of old, working with them in our context and taking them into the future. (If we didn't, who else would?) Same thing scientists, doctors, psychologists, and many other professionals do. Nothing would get done if individuals merely went along with established thought and never added to it. It's evolution, pure and simple.

The Church of Satan charges application fees for membership and further involvement and accepts money from people. Sounds like your garden-variety, tent-show, evangelist scam.

First off, you are probably confusing two different terms. The Church of Satan is an organization. Satanism is a religion. Since we are one of the few (if not one of the *only*) religions whose organized body *rejects* the tax exempt status other religions cling to, the CoS accepts money to keep it moving, and we pay *back* into the economic system. (This is but one manifestation of our ethic, "Responsibility to the responsible.") The money that the Church of Satan receives for its unsolicited memberships and fees goes to administrative costs, such as those incurred by any other organization. If a credible Satanist pays into the CoS, he or she does this in support, and does it with the mindfulness that any true Satanist possesses. You don't even have to be a member of the CoS to be a Satanist, so no money is required in that capacity, unlike that required by others for tithes, collection plates, and holy corn meal. The monetary fee, by extension, also keeps out most of the unwanted trend chaser and occult dabbler types.

I really want to join the Church of Satan... I mean, A LOT! I want to be a Priest and be one of you. I want magical powers and a direct phone-line to Satan.

The Church of Satan is an organization which recognizes worth in individuals based on actual achievement in the real world. Titles in the Church of Satan are strictly based on such concrete qualities, and are not achievements in and of themselves. Aside from Registered Membership, all Church of Satan titles are granted by appointment only and for which cannot be applied. This is, no doubt, of great dismay to those who wish to claim Satanic affiliation in an "official" sense yet lack personal success, direction, or influence upon their daily lives. Since we reject spirituality as patent nonsense, we are not interested in those chasing after occult monikers or access to some imaginary wellspring of magical power "out there." Further details on CoS hierarchical structure are at its official website.

As a representative for Satanism, you do interviews and lectures. Isn't this preaching? And, doesn't this violate your rule of not giving your opinions unless asked?

Of course this isn't preaching and it doesn't go against the First Satanic Rule of the Earth. If you open a magazine, turn on your radio, or click on your television and see an interview with a Satanist, you've reached a point where you will either not read or look at it, or you will. If you choose the latter, you have consigned yourself to the information and, by your own actions, have given your non-verbal consent to receive such information about our religion. If you attend a lecture, you have even more so welcomed yourself to our "opinions." No one coerced you to attend or read or watch or listen. Assuming that Satanism can be preached is to assume that anyone can be a Satanist, which is grossly false. We know this and wouldn't bother proselytizing like other religions. It would waste our time and we'd have to care, which we don't.

Can you tell me about (random diabolical myth figure from some ancient culture)?

Few ideologies stress more than Satanism the championing of self-assertiveness, of self-achievement and seeking things out for yourself, though most who ask the above question are not keeping that in mind. It is recommended that the aforementioned question should be refocused into making the effort to do the research on such yourself. If you ask this question to various Agents, Priests, and Magisters, don't be surprised if you are ignored. They're sending you the biggest hint they can, which is to find the info out for yourself.

After reading the FAQ and looking over your website, I want you to give me MORE. Would you answer my long list of questions?

If you have really read *The Satanic Bible* and related books, critically read some of our better magazines, and really paid attention to the websites with legitimate information on them, then you have *more* than enough of a jumpstart towards further knowledge. (What do you think those pre-Internet folks such as us did? We actually took the initiative and worked for what we know. Don't be surprised if we don't jump to your beck and call every time you have a question.) The rest is up to you. Apply what you know and see what happens. It is not the job of any CoS member or administrator to hold your hand and lead you down the Left Hand Path. That journey is a solitary one, as any true individual knows.

APPENDIX

IV. Suggested Reading

Atwood, Margaret. *The Handmaid's Tale*. New York: Fawcett Crest. 1985.
Barton, Blanche. *The Church of Satan*. New York: Hell's Kitchen Productions. 1990.
Barton, Blanche. *The Secret Life of a Satanist: The Authorized Biography of Anton LaVey*. Los Angeles: Feral House. 1990.
Bierce, Ambrose. *The Devil's Dictionary*. New York: Dover. 1993.
Bloom, Howard. *The Lucifer Principle*. New York: Atlantic Monthly Press. 1995.
Bradbury, Ray. *Fahrenheit 451*. New York: Ballantine. 1979.
Carnegie, Dale. *How To Win Friends and Influence People*. Revised Edition. New York: Simon and Schuster. 1981.
Conway, Flo and Jim Siegelman. *HOLY TERROR: The Fundamentalist War on America's Freedoms in Religion, Politics, and Our Private Lives*. Garden City, NY: Doubleday. 1982.
Dawkins, Richard. *The God Delusion*. New York: Houghton Mifflin Company. 2006.
Fritscher, Jack. *Popular Witchcraft (Second Edition)*. Madison, WI: University of Wisconsin Press. 2004.
Fussell, Paul. *Class: A Guide Through The American Status System*. New York: Touchstone. 1983.
Gilmore, Peter H. *The Satanic Scriptures*. Scapegoat Publishing. 2007.
Harris, Sam. *Letter To A Christian Nation*. New York: Alfred A. Knopf. 2006.
Henry, William A. III. *In Defense of Elitism*. New York: Anchor Books. 1994.
Hoffer, Eric. *The True Believer: Thoughts on the Nature of Mass Movements*. New York: HarperPerrenial. 1951.
King, Florence. *With Charity Toward None: A Fond Look At Misanthropy*. New York: St. Martin's Griffin. 1992.

LaVey, Anton Szandor. *The Devil's Notebook*. Portland, OR: Feral House. 1992.
LaVey, Anton Szandor. *The Satanic Bible*. New York: Avon. 1969.
LaVey, Anton Szandor. *The Satanic Rituals*. New York: Avon. 1972.
LaVey, Anton Szandor. *The Satanic Witch*. Los Angeles: Feral House. 1989.
LaVey, Anton Szandor. *Satan Speaks!*. Venice, CA: Feral House. 1998.
Levin, Ira. *Rosemary's Baby*. U.S: Fawcett Crest, 1967.
Liddy, G. Gordon. *WILL*. New York: St. Martin's Press. 1980.
London, Jack. *The Sea Wolf*. New York: Bantam Books. 1960.
Machiavelli, Niccolo. *The Prince*. New York: Knopf, Inc. 1992.
Mencken, H.L. *DAMN! A Book of Calumny*. New York: Philip Goodman. 1918.
Milton, John. *Paradise Lost*. Markham, Ontario, Canada: Mentor. 1961.
Morgan, Genevieve and Tom. *The Devil: A Visual Guide to the Demonic, Evil, Scurrilous and Bad*. San Francisco: Chronicle Books. 1996.
Nemo. *The Fire From Within: Nemo on Satanism Volume One*. Prometheus Foundation. 2007.
Nietzsche, Friedrich. *Thus Spoke Zarathustra*. New York: Penguin Books. 1961.
Nietzsche, Friedrich. *Twilight of the Idols/The Anti-Christ*. New York: Penguin. 1968.
Postman, Neil. *Amusing Ourselves To Death*. New York: Penguin Books. 1985.
Rand, Ayn. *Anthem (Centennial Edition)*. New York: Plume. 1999.
Redbeard, Ragnar. *Might Is Right*. Chicago: M.H.P. & Co., Ltd. 1996.
Russell, Bertrand. *Why I Am Not A Christian*. New York: Touchstone. 1957.
Simmons, Gene. *Sex Money KISS*. Beverly Hills: Simmons Books. 2003.
Starkey, Marion L. *The Devil In Massachusetts: A Modern Enquiry into the Salem Witch Trials*. New York: Anchor Books. 1949.
Turner, Alice K. *The History of Hell*. New York: Harcourt Brace. 1993.
Victor, Jeffrey S. *Satanic Panic: The Creation of a Contemporary Legend*. Chicago: Open Court. 1993.

APPENDIX

V. FROM THE MAIL BAG

[Having produced and released quite a bit of what is, in essence, Satanic media, I've received a great deal of mail, both in support and in protest of the work I do. Considering that it's the truly bizarre and loony ones that entertain, here are some choice bits, with all of the original typographical errors left in place for authenticity. - MGP]

Is that XXX as in sex rated? So somen women really get off on demonic art. My girlfriend is one of them. But good pornographic demonic art is hard to find. Am I looking in the right place? Something like a studly devil dog banging a young nymph or women and snake. Maybe you know of a source?

D. M.
Torrance, CA

P.S.: Don't know what happens at Satanic rituals but from what we have heard about Voo Doo sex rituals it sounds sexually exciting.

---

hi, i need your help! my wife has received the honor of being named the altar for her grotto and to recognize her achievement i would like to get her a special gift she has been wanting. i do not belong to her group and therefore am unable to ask for help from other members. please assist me. This required considerable work, study, acquiring several arrests for being available on the streets, and public display of Satanic devotion. She was competing against 2 other experienced women. i congratulate her efforts. More than anything i know of she would like to have a wooden crucifix dildo with her name and status engraved in it. i can not find one anywhere. for the past three years she has used at home a regular wooden cross that i planed round for her. Now she is to provide hers for the Mass. Where can i get it for her? Also, she practices many acts of christian defilement at home but, i know she would appreciate being able to expand. currently she (i assist) celebrates a home version of the mass, afterwards she pisses into the wine wipes her vagina with the host and dumps them into the toilet shitting on them praising Satan. She uses the bible as toilet paper. Has written the infernal names on the attic ridgeboard in our house. placed her confirmation cross into a jar of her urine. and one of her favorites every year is celebrating shitmas on dec25. She places a nativity set into a bucket then shits on it. We are both 40 years old so her devotion is not a teenage fancy or college prank. We would be grateful for additional rituals and source of her dildo. we are new to the internet only signing on last month so we also are in need of site addresses.

PentaCasa

---

hi my name is steve im 13 and have been a satanist for 2 years. i need some help. i belive that satanism isnt just a philosophy. i belive there is a being that is satan and that there are lots of demons. i have asked satan to help me with things that are pretty hard to help with but without a doubt he was there and helped me. now i have 2 questions. am i a satanist??? and could you give me some directions on how to make conntact with a demon?????

thank you -- steve

---

okay you say that Satanist are MATURE whatever. on your stupid thing about FAQ you were like being dumb and sarcastic and guess what immature. isnt that a quawinkidink!!!! guess what.... you also had some crap about umm....... the difference between devil worship and satan worship duh!!!! satan and the devil are the same LOSERS! ne ways dont be dissin christians im one and also satan was banished from heaven b/c he was sooo pridful yet your teaching it guess what your all going to hell and let me tell ya sunny boy hell aint no sauna lol. get a clue. oh yeah i know why your reaching out to youth im infact 15 just this tuesday if your depressed self wanted to know lol. neways you are reaching out to youth because we are in the stage of adolecence and rebellion......we are the most impresionable. i love GOD you cant change me and i cant make you and your hell bus fair stop but i can tell ya that satan is NOT ne where near kind and will never be also in your crap that you wrote!

about what satan is......from what i read you and satan need to go to anger management classes. lol get the facts straight and while your at it get a reall life. k. also you worship the DEVIL AKA. SATAN b/c you dont want to submit to some one who is way better than you GOD. you want to be your own god and if thats what you think you are then you are living in fantasy world and you need to wake up lol high priest of the church of the devil my butt!!! lol also while your burnin in hell for eternity ill be drinkin lemonade lol you betcha!!! have a nice "IM GOING TO HELL" day lol :) bu bye see ya later.....actually i hope i dont opps lol :)

graves

I know what goes on in your evil underground Satanic Covens. Rapers, child molesters, ritual murders. Well your time has come. I'm compiling a full report and handing you all over to the FBI. And you thought you could get away with all your hedious inhumane crimes! Your all going to get the electric chair for this. Mark my words.

Robert.

---

hi. i dont know how to write this but i respect you. im a devout Christian, but i am interested in learning about satanism to fight him. im going to do research some more. im only 15, but since i will know alot about Satan and i know about God, i will be able to fight you. You have contributed valuable information to me. I hope Satan is after me more than ever. If he has a hit list, i hope i am at the top of the list and highlighted. Thank you for contributing your efforts to bring your people down. If you have anything to say to me, please email me back and tell me that im wrong. i want you to tell me that im wrong. I want you to know that you and Satan should be very VERY scared of the Christians right now. We are far more dangerous than anyone with an atomic bomb, let alone Satan. I think its amazing that Spiritual warfare is going on in my room right this very minute. Is it happening in your room, too? I hope so. May Satan help you, and I know he will. You're already putty in his hands. That's why he wants me more than he wants you. But he will never have me. Jealous?

Chuck

---

he die saturday at 11:45pm I want all hes memoris in my soul today monday. because hes soul whil go today!

joselb2

My name is [name deleted]. I am 52 and live in Ontario, California. I want to know how I can become a Satanic Priest. I will be going into truck driving school in 2 weeks and I would like to study while on the road. Thank you.

---

hello Matt,
it's a pleasure writing you today, infact i have been trying all my possible best to be fully linked and become a life membetr of this church of satan but i doesn't have the membership fine to offer ($208). am desperatly looking a way to belong and start up with people and to achieve all my focus needs to life. i would be glad if you can do something.

---

thank you for the info. mr paradise i am a big fan of yours and sincerly complement you on your soccess! is it possible to send me an aplication for membership for c.o.s..dr.lavey has been a positive and fruitful influence in my life and i very much would like to become a member. mr paradise if you have any literature or any kind of corospondance please send any or all to my home address mr. h.g.b. jr. [home address deleted] mr.paradise im sure you are very busy i just seek corospondance with other satanist because where i live true satanist are few and fae between.

again i am a fan of your workand thank you for your time. A.S.XL 01 05 HAIL SATAN H.B. CAN YOU TELL ME HOW OLD XERXES IS AND IF HE WILL ASSUME DR. LAVEYS PLACE.

HELP ME PLS I WANT TO BE UR SON IN THE GREAT CHURCH OF SATAN PLS MY LORD HELP ME TO ACTIVE WHT I WHEN TO ACTIVE FOR THE GREAT MASTER.

HENRY

Dear Matt,

I get the marvelous impression u r erotic and a good writer, your website is fun with, a dash of eroticism, well done. I would love a nude center fold of you can you please send one or more to me, please.

Gordon

---

hail satan!
hello
this is just an email from a 16 year old girl in hobart, tasmania, australia, I am looking for information on joining the official satanic scene, i have been an un-official member for the past 5 years but feel it is time to join the official dark side!
I attend an australian christian school, Hartridge christian school. where everyone is very closed minded and will not accept my way of satanic living and beliefs.
It is impossible to move to a different school as as this is the only on in an hour radius of my house.
I suffer great hurt from my class mates who are filled with negative, false stereotypes of our kind, of sacrifice and virgin raping.
How can i make them see the light of my dark ways?
Help me sir, satan in kind.
I have preformed may rituals but i am beginning to lose faith in satan, why does he not appear when i summon his courage? am i too weak for him?
please help me.

I am loosing my faith in great satan
if you have any pamphlets or books to help me regain my faith
please help me
regards Mystic
hail satan!

I am here to tell what you are missing! You are missing a full life of love and trust in your true father! God loves you with all his heart and if you do not accept him into yours, you will hurt inside because all of that pain you let burn there. Jesus Christ volunteered to die for you 1 thousand years ago, so what will you lose? If I am wrong then I go nowhere when I die, but if you are, then at least you will know... Please think of a fulfilled life in love with your true father, God.

In God's love, Sean

Hi,

Seeing the Adam Family videos 1991-93 the years I went to high school and graduated 93 brought back such memories. It all happened in New Jersey were I think the daughter/actress Ricci was born. Such memories of Tombstone/the town that stopped in 1881 and is being studied by freemasonry as is the traditions since the American Revolution of all our SPECIAL FORCES of the military. And in this specific case Military Intelligence in the nearby Fort Hug something. Key West has the Navy Seals. My younger brother was born in 1981. And nearby Tucson well my fathers name begin with Tor. And Arizona/so appropriate as a state for the Adam's. In my case the original family name was Asbjornsen. So in this paradise for nazists, the state of Arizona/USS ARIZONA sank in Pearl Harbor, also were pentagrams/hexagrams of witchcraft. Me a unique character/person in a state where they needed something unique to get tourism to the ghost towns. Imagine the dreams to run your own little ghost town on behalf of owners. And you yourself being the main attraction etc. So much from the modern Adam's Family film obviously represents all we know about the Church of Satan from the current published materials. It was with a sense of cynicism that I read that everything was fictious at the end of the Hollywood feature. Yet horror has so much to give. It develops human beings. I don't know where America would be without street performers/theater etc. Without our special forces/intelligence truly our military would forget very much of its history and civilization. These particular versions of the Adam's Family are well calculated in the details of evil/opposite of good. Horror truly is more important even than sex. And hence from horror we can learn to deal with puberty. But much more through theater/acting we can learn about humanity. Where indeed would relationships be without us trying to hurt/scare/give pain to each other or rather witchcraft and evil emotions. We depend upon the practice of evil from our partners in order to survive in America/the free market etc. Hell/devils are all real for the most part. Through evil we can learn about our enslavement to evil in the society.... Well anyhow such is my faith. There are very many reasons why Arizona is the Paradise of Nazism. They can't afford not to socialize. They are fact oriented and very impressionable. Everyone is very intelligent. And they are extremly conservative in a geopolitical environment that is bohemian/paraphernilia etc. It is beyond me how these Arizona people don't have any sense of being controlled by the government etc. It is like the civilian part of the military districts. Nature is the controlling influence. What I didn't like about the Adam's Family new film version was that he was Spanish characteristic and she was French speaking. As if FRANCE had not been the only and most great country for emotional intelligence development. As if both genders unhindered from nuclear family control didn't deserve France equally etc. Geopolitics I suppose. Provider need to know the border language. - C.O.

Hello Matt, as a fellow satanist I feel you need punchment for you sin. I would have taken you to the basement just before dinner time and, pulled your pants and, shorts down and, put you over my Knee and, given you an, old fashion spanking to get the bad out of you. Then send you upstare for a nice dinner with me sitting across the table from you. This is exactly what you need.

R.B.
[home telephone number deleted]

Can i introduce myself to you i'm Nnamdi okafor a NIGERIAN living in Anambra state in the town of Awelle.I have been hedem for a long time for some years back, so like four years back i started a followship i called order of satan at a time i was looking forward to get a counsellor but i later got a man who started teaching me all about satan but later i got a book called seven wonders of the world and one other book i borrowed i started using it in my teaching in the followship and we where about 47 that was in april 2003 and we were doing the followship in one place we rented but later in october i found out your church i mean church of satan so i decided to write you people to know wheather you will be giving me counselling online as in sending it to my e-mail box[e-mail address deleted] but i couldn't get your e-mail address till i browsed it and found it so that's why i'm writing now to know wheather you can do it for me.

Again in the area i started the followship the people around it majority are hedems so i decided to make our followship a church then i wanted to know if in any way you people can help me finiancially so that i can buy a land and also build a modern church here as making the followship a church and also since you have the same thing in mind with me in the exitance of satan i decied to write to know if you can help in any little way so that we can call the church [church of satan] so that we can have a branch in the area i'm talking about because i know how many souls we have won since we started with order of satan i know if we build a church and call it by the name church of satan we will win more soul more than we're thinking so after the my though i costed every thing that 're going to be needed in project it arise at the sum of USD 70,000 [seventy thousand united states dollars] so how do we do it to get the support from you because i know with your support we can have your church here,like i said that we are going to change the followship to church of satan if you give us the money needed for the project.But i'm not trying to force but as a spiritualist intrested in the work of satan and spreding of the word throughout that area i strongly belief that you people can do it so that we can have the branch over here.But i heard from my congregation that there's already a branch in Enugu Nigeria but i can't locate the place so if you can give me the address so that i can go and locate them since we're about to be the same.

Finally i will like you to forward this to any strong member of the church so we will know what they can donate toward this project but if you can't why not send like some e-mail address of some members so that i can write them myself and tell them what i have in mind.

Thanks as you co-operate with us

                    Yours strongly beliver of exitance of satan
                                Nnamdi Okafor

Dear Sir Reverend Matt Paradise,

I extend to you nocturnal greetings and many howls and hails. I'm not really sure as to if I should address you as "Father" or not because you are a priest after all, no? Should I recount/confess to you My sins? Trust Me, I will at your request.<grins evilly>

So, how are you? Okay, so much for formal introductions, it has finally flown out the window. As for Me, well, I'm...surviving, you know, trying to deal and cope with the stupidity of Man on a daily basis while trying to maintain My sanity all at once.<exasperated sigh>

How goes it at CoS? Forgive Me as I really don't have much to asy or maybe I do I just...I don't know, maybe feel you out a bit by responding to My E-Mail.<grins>

Well anyway, I hope to hear from you soon and I hope that you do write back. So...um..see you later, I guess. Bye.<runs away with her tail between her legs>

In Darkness and Shadows,
Mistress Black-Moon>;[

---

by first impression, it is difficult to know which direction to take with the 'Church of Satan'...i have only briefly heard of the 'working of Satan today', although i am sure there is valid proof with such a 'following'... i have been in San Francisco several times, and i know it is 'brothing over' with activity, and i have remained a 'stranger' to the city, and the activities of the 'Church of Satan' there...got any suggestions?... [e-mail address deleted] there, it may be rewarding to frequent there, or in other cities, and provide a way to encounter 'active men, and women', 'socially responsible', and other groups at such a place...i have an off and on friend from san francisco who is a warlock, and suggests that there ought to be such a place called 'the sorcerors tea', and in order to meet active people or groups from this religion, his name is Desmond, some say he goes by 'Mars', if you know anyone interested in this type of capital venture please get in touch as soon as possible, and if you know of Desmond, please contact...i am still trying to find out how to contact him, and have show up in person, and to fulfill and complete these outstanding plans and purposes, and for this remarkable city of san francisco, and others...the money is good, and a worthwhile project...Desmond needs the money too...he says he is a sorceror, and i don't really believe him.... if you hear from him, let me know....kd

---

Hi there

I am wishing to join the 'cult' as people call it of satanism. i wondered what exactaliy does this mean, do i have to comit myself to do anything. many people wear a cross. but i have seen satanists wearing a gold cross upside down, do you have to do this or can you just wear it the normal way.

please help in any way you can
thanks

Every time, that I come in to your website(everyday) ,
I see you...and all these feelings, just ....I can't explain.
I am sorry to bother you again.
But my morningstar is you again.
You drive me crazy, I am going wild
all this emotions. make me feel extremetly arouse.
It is me onces again, I could not even imagine,
how good you taste in bed.
Not just as s lust feeling , but as person as well.
I want to know about you, if you let me in,
You are the feeling of desire as much as an intelligent man.
I wan't to see at least, some words from you, that you undrstand.
That your, eyes, your personality, your class, yourself , your knowledge
and you as a normal man,
are making me feel like a woman. for the 1st time.
You have make me feel like noone before,
and I dont't even have speak a word or see you at all.

I know, you may get a lots of these, so forgive me if I bother you.

Please, at least let me know.
do you wan't me to stop?
Please tell me.
I will as soon as you tell me.
"Your will is my law"

N.O.

Dear Matt, Found your website the other night. Strange, because I had been praying all day for God to set free ALL those involved in Satanism/Luciferianism...and THEN I find your website! Glad I did, dear. I will add your name to those for whom I pray constantly for DELIVERANCE from Satanism, and to find true peace within through the REAL light of Illumination, Jesus Christ.

    I know Satanism does NOT work. My dad was a part of the well known DC SATANIST ELITE. Very famous in the DC area, even posthumously. But his recruitment into SATANISM brought hell into our home as I grew up (no pun intended.)

    I had to turn to JESUS CHRIST to save me from my cruel Satanist father. and THAT is when I discovered FIRST HAND the REAL power of Jesus Christ over Satanism! What LOVE, what POWER came into my life through Jesus Christ. And thirty years later, my dad became a CHRISTIAN. he admitted SATANISM DID NOT WORK, and repented for all the evil he had done with other Satanist elite for many years, worldwide in rituals.

    And what a miraculous transformation Jesus Christ brought into his life! Years of torment, guilt, flashbacks and more were washed away as he turned to the GREATER God, and obtained deliverance from the destroying torment of LUCIFER/SATAN...

    Honey, with what is coming to our nation, you are going to need GREATER POWER than His Evilness could EVER give you. Jesus Christ stands at the door of YOUR heart to love you, forgive you, empower you and SET YOU FREE.

    I don't care HOW MANY human sacrifices you've done, how many times you THINK you've "crossed the line" and "God could NEVER forgive me...if there IS a god..." the TRUTH is, Jesus Christ died on the cross to TAKE THE RAP for you and all the nasty things you've EVER done, so that YOU CAN BE FORGIVEN. Remember that when He was nailed to the Cross, it was by ROMAN PAGANS.. He WAS a human sacrifice! But what did He say o God about those who made Him into a human sacrifice??? "Father FORGIVE THEM, for they KNOW NOT WHAT THEY DO!" "NOT "BURN 'em," or "DAMN 'em," but rather "FORGIVE THEM."...

You're on my prayer list, dear!

(h, and by the way, I know all about coming MARTIAL LAW and Satan's nasty little DAWNING OF THE NEW WORLD ORDER agenda to TERMINATE THE CHRISTIANS with cutesy little termination tools like the concentration camps, the guillotines, the boxcars and shackles and more. Any Satanist worth their title knows about this..so I guess you do too. But you know what???NONE OF THESE TOOLS OF TERMINATION can move me from my faith in the GREATER GOD, Jesus Christ. I would rather die for Jesus Christ, than GO TO HELL for Satan. Think about it, dear....

Love in my Jesus, Pamela

Greetings! Rev.Matt......

I took the liberty to glaze inside your website.
I felt so touch and amaze, on the way that you talk about your mother.
I felt, intrigued, about the way, you wrote.
An unusual attraction towards your pictures, the power of your writing and feelings of lust, took place inside myself.
Your sense of knowledge and experience,took over my mind, in the amount of minutes that I spent in your website.
You are a very intelligent man, with great communication skills as well.
Sensitive to the arts, and respectful when it comes to woman.
Fair and committed, responsible and strong.
Your overpowering personality , encourage me to believe.
Believe that there are not many people as beautiful as you.
You are the must sensual, attractive, intelligent human .
I dont know, how to explain, that your taste, class and unique, personality, allowed me to tell you all this things.
Knowing that perhaps, you may not even read my e-mail,
I decided to take the risk and approach you.
I hope that you dont feel bother by my comments.

I will like to introduce my self.
I am J.C.D.
I am 27 years old
I am not a Satanist,
I am very similar, and fascinated with you.
I will attach a picture, so you know who I am.
I will be delighted If you reply my e-mail.
At least, if you are ever up to conversation, let me know.
I wont say it will be an honor.
But I will say that , I will feel flattered.And i will say that I wont let you waist your time.
Maybe you will like to talk about an old fascinating book or perhaps about yourself.

With all my respect....

I thought that 'CoS Reject' title might catch your eye-all though I don't feel like a reject. :p I was, however, denied membership with the CoS.

     I was wondering, could you give me insights as to why my membership application was rejected? I received no reply from the CoS-only a return through paypal.
     I will not attempt to change myself to fit the CoS mold. I value myself much more than having membership with any organization that I admire.
     Despite this, I am dying to know why I wasn't granted membership. I never doubted I'd 'get in'. It seemed like a perfect match. I'm thinking the reason (s) could possibly be:

1. I used to lead my own satanic org-Gilmore had told me membership in both groups wouldn't jive with him-so I then decided to give up the [name of group deleted] (my old group) as an official organization.

2. I used to be a leader in a christian org as a young adult-maybe that's a bit scary for some?

I posted my CoS app here FYI (personal info excluded) [URL deleted]

If it interests you, please respond. I'd love to read your insights.

Paradise~

I believe in arcane power. I believe even though I know nothing of it. I have never directly been faced with it, nor observed another wielding it. I believe because I need to believe, I believe despite a lack of evidence, because it is inside me to believe. My heart knows what my head cannot confirm.

I am compelled. With respect, I come to you in desperation. Not a desperation of means, of literal life. I have no physical need for power, nor dilemna I cannot manage. I am desperate within. I am filled with melancholy. As I am now I know, I am not right. I am not complete. I refuse to accept the teachings around me, when they so drastically conflict with the tug of my heart.

I fear mediocrity. I fear acceptance of blandishment and lies. I know there is something wrong. The current picture, what I do see, what I can confirm...it's killing me. Slowly, but killing me all the same.

There was a time when mages counciled kings.

I want to know.

What do I do?

Abel

So...if you have anything left in that black heart of yours,would you send me something wich could make me understand satanists?Well...I don't belive in God or something,so I eighter belive in the devil.And I certainly don't understand satanists,tough I like their signs, I like to see blood and I like all the scary tales told by them.
All I want is information.I'm very confused and sometimes I'm afraid that if the demons are real,they could get inside me...
I need to know what you know!
Please,give me these informations.I want to know all that made you become satanists!

Please answer me!

A young man with thirst of knowledge.

I have an antique bed that is rather unique and would like to find out some info on it. I believe it is mahogany? and I swear it is possessed. The size is a full bed with a head board and a footboard. The headboard is over 5 ft tall and the design that is in the wood actually looks like some sort of demon head with eyes. It appears to be the grain of the wood and is very prominent. It is actually very spooky looking. There is also two side profiles of this same face. It appears to have wings or claws on it as well. There is a matching dresser with a large mirror that has side shelves. The dresser has a marble top. The only dates I can find on the bed are in the locks on the drawers and they are 1873 and 1882.

This bed was purchased in Michigan from a dealer in 1965. Have you ever heard of such a bed? I have never seen anything like it. Thank you

APPENDIX

VI. MGP Media Resume

Audio
-- Bassist/Vocalist for numerous bands (1984-1992)
-- Band Manager and Booking Agent for regional music acts (1986-1987)
-- Sound Engineer for numerous band demos and live shows (1986-1992)
-- Production Manager, WJSC 90.7 FM (1990-1992)
-- Metal Director, WJSC 90.7 FM (1990-1992)
-- DJ/Producer of "The Slam Compactor" (1990-1992) - radio show
-- DJ/Producer of "Captain Thrash and the Straight Edge Kid Hour" (1991-1992) - radio show
-- DJ/Producer of "Hell's Closet" (1991-1992) - radio show
-- DJ/Co-producer of "Poo Poo Radio" (1994-1996) - radio show
-- Producer of The Purging Talon Vault Tapes CD (2000)
-- Producer of There's Nothing You Can Do: Pubic Itch (1984-1989) CD (2000)
-- Host/Producer of Heavy Metal Memories (2003-2006) - Internet radio show
-- Production on select promos and I.D.s for radiofreesatan.com (2003-2006)

Print
-- Columnist of "The Fifth Angle" in The Simplectic (1991-1992)
-- Editor/Publisher of Poo Poo Magazine (1993-1998)
-- Columnist for The ROC (notably, issues 11-13; early- to mid-'90s)
-- Editor/Publisher of Not Like Most (1995-present)
-- Editor/Publisher of the print version of Superhighway To Hell

(2000-2003)
-- Editor/Publisher of The Book of Satanic Quotations (1st ed., 2002)

Video
-- Numerous show I.D.s, bumpers, promos, and other video elements for personal projects (1997-present)
-- Producer of Subterranean SINema (1997-?) - public access television show
-- Producer of "Studio 8 Unmasked" (1998) - mockumentary on "Studio 8 Live," a former public access TV show
-- Producer of "Cusco: A Visual Account" (1999) - documentary short on a trip to Peru
-- Producer of "How To Make Chainmaile" (1999) - instructional video
-- Producer of Satanism Today (The Video Version; 2002-2006) - public access television show
-- Producer of The Church of Satan Interview Archive DVD (2003)
-- Producer of Satanism Today Volume One DVD (2003)
-- Producer of Satanism Today Volume Two DVD (2003)
-- Producer of "Big Heavy World: Attention Bands" video promo (2003)
-- Producer of The Best of Subterranean SINema DVD (2004)
-- Producer of "Under The Surface: The Legend of Subterranean SINema" (2004) - documentary / DVD featurette
-- Producer of The Purging Talon Video Sampler DVD (2004)
-- Producer of numerous ".com" promos (2004-present)
-- Producer of "Battle Hymn of the Apocalypse" (2005) - music video for Le' rue Delashay

www.ingramcontent.com/pod-product-compliance
Lightning Source LLC
Chambersburg PA
CBHW022102160426
43198CB00008B/315